Fine Wine
and a
Midlife Crisis

Tara Freeman

This book is dedicated to all the women who helped make the bad times bearable and the good times memorable. They know who they are.

Published by ASSH Publishing 2014

Copyright © 2014 Theresa Charles

All rights reserved. No part of this publication may be reproduced, stored in a retrieval system, or transmitted in any form or by any means, electronic, mechanical, photocopying, recording or otherwise, without the prior written permission from the publisher.

A catalogue record for this book is available from the National Library of Australia.

Book cover design and formatting services by BookCoverCafe.com

www.gidgeebaskets.com

First Edition 2014

ISBN:
978-0-9925496-0-2 (pbk)
978-0-9925496-1-9 (ebk)

Contents

Introduction		v
Chapter 1	Childhood	7
Chapter 2	My Father	9
Chapter 3	My Mother	16
Chapter 4	Nursing	19
Chapter 5	Travel	28
Chapter 6	The Proposal	43
Chapter 7	The Wedding	47
Chapter 8	My Husband	53
Chapter 9	Soul Mates	62
Chapter 10	Sex	65
Chapter 11	Masturbation	70
Chapter 12	Pregnancy and Babies	74
Chapter 13	Our Children	90
Chapter 14	Motherhood	99
Chapter 15	Brawling Kids	107
Chapter 16	Kids and Shopping	110
Chapter 17	Road Trips with Kids	115

Chapter 18	Housework	125
Chapter 19	Cooking	127
Chapter 20	Homework	131
Chapter 21	Bathtime	133
Chapter 22	Bedtime	135
Chapter 23	School Holidays	138
Chapter 24	School Mums	141
Chapter 25	Coffee Groups	143
Chapter 26	Relatives	145
Chapter 27	Family Holidays	147
Chapter 28	Friends	149
Chapter 29	Appearances	157
Chapter 30	Exercise	159
Chapter 31	Facebook and other Social Media	163
Chapter 32	Parties	169
Chapter 33	Doctors' Appointments	177
Chapter 34	Women's Health	179
Chapter 35	Television	181
Chapter 36	Reading	184
Chapter 37	Small Towns	186
Chapter 38	The Arts	188
Chapter 39	Committees	191
Chapter 40	My Gift Shop	193
Chapter 41	Giving Presents	198
Chapter 42	Surgery	200
Chapter 43	Travelling with the In-laws	205
Chapter 44	Chaos and the Big Kids	207
Chapter 45	Personal Space	209
Chapter 46	Musings	214
Acknowledgements		220

Introduction

OMG, I'm turning forty. How is that possible? It doesn't seem that long ago that I was eighteen and thought forty was old and way too far in my future to worry about. Now those intervening years have gone, as though I've lost my keys, which actually happened to me the other day, but that's a story for another book.

I wonder if my real identity has been lost amidst becoming a wife, having children, and all of society's other demands. Or am I still the person I should be? Could I still be the same fun-loving, hot, sexy, desirable and drop-dead gorgeous woman I really want to be in my dreams?

It's always been my goal to write a book before my fortieth birthday. I began recording my thoughts and my life story when I turned thirty-nine and the reality of actually turning forty was coming towards me like a steam train. I had to attempt to do this while I was still in my thirties, as for some bizarre reason I thought that I might not be able to the day after I was no longer thirty-nine.

My purpose in writing this book is to reveal real emotions and be totally honest. Above all else, I want my book to be honest. I want women to be able to read it and think, OMG, I feel that way too, but I've never been able to admit to it.

I want to tell the story of what one woman really thinks and feels. We women tend to just get on with life, to keep up appearances and give the impression that all is plain sailing and life is so damn wonderful. If just one person reads this, laughs and thinks, hell, yes, I can relate to that, my life will be complete.

1

Childhood

I was born into a regular working-class family in a small town in Far North Queensland. My mother is a nurse and my father was a salesyard clerk in the local council. He had worked for the town council since he was sixteen, and my mother has been nursing since she was seventeen.

During my formative years they both encouraged me to live by the old-fashioned core values of responsibility for my own actions, strong work ethic, and respect for other people, which has carried me in good stead throughout my life. I have many fond memories of my childhood, but some sad memories as well.

I'm grateful to my parents for introducing me to the wonders of travel at a very young age. We first went overseas on a family holiday when I was just three years of age. They had always wanted to travel and the fact they had a small child was no impediment to their plans. We went on another trip overseas when

I was ten years old and my younger sister, Megan, was three. By that age I was more aware and appreciative of the varying cultures and some of the history of the countries we visited, and those trips started my lifelong passion for travel.

My parents divorced and my father's mother died in the same year, so at the tender age of eleven I lost the two most significant female influences in my life. I didn't see it at the time, as I was too devastated by my loss, but I can look back now and appreciate the strength I developed from both those events.

Megan and I stayed with our dad. I had to grow up very quickly and help take care of my five-year-old baby sister. Overnight I left my carefree childhood behind. I did my best to share household responsibilities and help my dad wherever I could. I started taking on babysitting jobs when I was twelve, and by the time I was thirteen I had three part-time jobs.

What I've learned from my formative years is that life is rarely perfect, and childhood passes much too quickly. Even though we all do endure losses, we should never forget that overall it's great being a kid. All of life's lessons are character building. We should always focus on the positives, and move onto the next phase of our lives with courage to do the best we can with what we have.

2

My Father

The greatest gift my father gave me was his belief in me. As a father, my dad was very patient. He was someone who 'got' me. Not many people really get you in life, and if you're lucky enough to have experienced such a relationship, it's such a wonderful thing to cherish. My father died before I had my children, a terrible loss as he would have made a great grandfather.

Dad was someone who quietly got on with his life and would do the most thoughtful things without being asked. When I finally moved away from home, he would turn up at my flat with extra food and make out it was 'leftovers' from dinner, but I always knew it was something he had prepared especially for me.

One day when I was making idle conversation with him I mentioned that my partner James, who would later become my husband, had been given a breadmaker. When I got home from work, there was bread mix sitting at my front door, courtesy of my dad.

And because he had to bring up two girls, Dad was familiar with the ways of us females. One day at the hospital where I worked as a nurse I was suffering from a urinary tract infection, didn't make it to the toilet in time and had a wee accident. I phoned my dad, who was also at work. He went home and grabbed me some clean underpants.

My work colleagues and friends were always amazed at what he would do for me. On another occasion, one of the other nurses had a menstrual accident. I phoned Dad and asked if he would be kind enough to bring in some feminine hygiene products. I made out they were for me.

'Are they those bullet-looking things?' he asked.

I assured him he was correct and, sure enough, he brought them in. My work colleague could not believe my father would do that for me, but that's the sort of person he was.

One morning I came home from night duty and there was Dad, sitting in the kitchen having his tea and toast with a magazine in front of him. After wishing me a good morning, he mentioned an article he had just finished reading on vaginal thrush. Apparently eating natural yoghurt helps, he told me. I was tired and needed to get to sleep, and could hardly focus on my father trying to discuss my vaginal-thrush concerns.

I could phone my father at any time and ask him to pick me up from the pub. Without hesitation, he would come down and collect my friends and me. One day James, who wasn't even my boyfriend at the time, asked my dad to pick him up after a night on the town.

2 MY FATHER

One evening I came home with a group of friends in the early hours of the morning. We were hungry, so my dad cooked homemade chips for us—*at three am*.

Some years ago, after a bachelor and spinster ball, a friend who was staying at our house got a lift home with the local police. The next morning she told me my dad had been hanging clothes on the line when she got home at three-thirty in the morning. 'When does he sleep?' she asked.

That's just how Dad was. As he got older he didn't require much sleep. If I were out on the town, he would usually stay up until I got home and he knew all was well.

I must have inherited Dad's genetic defect of not needing as much sleep as most people. I probably average between five and six hours a night. He never suffered from hangovers, and neither do I, much to the extreme annoyance of my husband and friends, who suffer for days after a good night out.

My father died within two weeks of being diagnosed with cancer. It was all very quick, and the nurse in me was pleased he didn't suffer for long, but the daughter in me wanted more time with him.

Dad had been feeling unwell and coughing for a while. He was a smoker and occasionally got chest infections. I didn't suspect anything initially but then his back began aching. Every night I would rub liniment into it. I still had no suspicion he was so ill, but one fateful day a woman who had moved away from our small town came back to visit and commented on how much weight he had lost.

At that exact moment everything fell into place and I knew, I just knew, that Dad had the big C. It was like time stood still. There I stood in the grocery store, and my worst nightmare was descending upon me. My wonderful, amazing, patient father had cancer.

I had a great battle on my hands to get him to the doctor, as he was a typical older-generation male. His own dad was the same; they both thought they had no need to go to the doctor. After much emotional blackmail on my part, he did finally go. The doctor checked his prostate and ran blood tests, and told him that everything appeared to be fine. Thinking all was okay, he and my sister Megan drove to the Sunshine Coast to spend time with Dad's youngest sister Bella and her family. I couldn't go with them, as I had to work.

On Christmas morning I walked into work just as the night-duty sister was walking out. She used to work at the medical clinic in town as well as the hospital. With no emotion at all, she told me that my father's blood tests were abnormal, suggesting he had cancer.

I managed to hold it together and phoned Aunty Bella, who I am very close to, and asked her to get my dad to a doctor ASAP. She was able to get a medical appointment for him straight after Boxing Day. The X-rays showed three masses on his lungs, and he also had a fractured spine where the cancer had metastasised into his bones. They didn't do any biopsies at that stage, just the X-rays.

Dad phoned me with the results and I couldn't speak. He kept saying, 'It's going to be okay, isn't it? It's nothing serious.'

I reassured him as best as I could, without dissolving into floods of tears. I couldn't speak by this stage, and when Aunty Bella came back on the line I had to hand the phone to James.

My father was in extreme pain with his back, but his actions then show the calibre of the man; the sheer determination that illustrates just a small part of this gentle giant's character. He drove from the Sunshine Coast all the way home to our small town in Far North Queensland, a distance of nearly two thousand kilometres. He wanted to be home on New Year's Day and no one could change his mind. I think he knew he was going to die and he needed to be in his precious hometown, and to have both of his daughters by his side.

On the way home he and Megan stayed one night at my grandma's near Rockhampton, and he was in so much pain he sat upright in a lounge-room chair, getting very little sleep. Megan had to drive for the next twelve hours to get him back home.

The minute he arrived I had him admitted to hospital. I can still picture the look on the face of one of the registered nurses at staff handover. I couldn't hear what was being said, but she looked around at me and it was a look of utter sorrow and sadness. Deep down, she knew as well as I did that Dad was dying.

This was 1999, the New Year's Eve entering the new millennium, and I spent it at the local lookout with James and our Jack Russell-crossbred dog, Molly. People were celebrating this momentous occasion throughout the world. Some were anticipating the crash of computers and all sorts of technical dramas, while others like me were contemplating tragedies that had entered their lives. The days that followed would be the most devastating of my life, and I have experienced my share of loss.

Dad was never a person for much fuss. On the morning of the day he died, I phoned all of his five siblings and told them he was slipping away. As a nurse, I knew the signs. Three siblings bought plane tickets although they couldn't get immediate flights, and his younger brother caught the next bus from Brisbane.

I felt such empathy for them, as they tried so hard to get to him in time to say their goodbyes. My poor uncle who was travelling by bus was given the news of Dad's passing by a minister at one of the bus stops along the way. His wife had managed to contact the church in that town and the minister kindly conveyed the sad news.

I asked Dad to wait for them. When someone is dying they're usually waiting for someone to arrive before they're at peace enough to move onto the next world, but I knew what my dad was thinking: *Not on your life am I hanging around for people to be fussing over me. I have my two girls either side of me and I'm all set.*

Like any parent, my dad had his faults. None of us are perfect, but as his daughter I wouldn't have wanted any other father.

An example of how he always thought of others first was the day I accidentally ran over our dog Molly the day before Dad died. I had driven under our flat, not realising she was tied up, and her lead got caught in the tyres of the ute. I was crying on the phone to a friend when Dad overheard me and asked if I was okay. He said he knew how upset I must be feeling.

At that point I was jolted straight back to the reality of my dad's situation. He was dying, but he was concerned about me crying over my dog. My priorities shifted real quick.

He passed away in hospital ten days after New Year's Eve, although we had managed to care for him at home until the night before he died.

On his headstone are the words: *You are our world, and the love of our life.*

What I've learned from my dad's style of parenting is the importance of patience, humility and communication. I could talk to him about anything (except of course sex; what father wants to know about that?). I've also learned to always expect the unexpected because we never know what life will throw at us. We think our parents are going to be around forever. No one else in our lives ever knows or understands us so completely. The relationships we share with our parents form the basis of all relationships we have in the future.

3

My Mother

How do I start to describe my mother? She has a very complex personality. After my parents separated I chose to live with my dad. It was a very simple choice for me. I loved my room; it was my sanctuary. And I was a daddy's girl.

This didn't mean I didn't love my mother, but she was very strict and her form of discipline would probably be considered child abuse today.

When I was about three or four years old, I decided to play with matches. Mum came into the bedroom and saw the bedspread alight. She turned on the stove hotplate and burnt my finger to teach me about the dangers of playing with fire, and then put cream on it afterwards to help soothe the burn. I can't light matches or lighters to this day.

As a child, I hated to have my hair in pigtails, as they were always within Mum's reach to pull me back and flog me.

I will say that today she never tries to deny her parenting methods. She says her discipline made me the person I am today and claims I turned out a better person for it.

Mum is an extremely hard worker. She has been a nurse for fifty years and at times even worked other jobs on her days off. When she was nursing in another Far North Queensland town some years ago, I had to have my wisdom teeth removed under a general anaesthetic. In those days there was a private hospital nearby and an orthodontist used to fly there from Brisbane to treat people in the Outback. My mum worked for two weeks straight to pay for the procedure. She also kept me on her private health insurance until I finished school.

She is not a soft and cuddly type of grandmother. I'm sure that deep down she loves our kids, but most of the time they annoy her. She says she almost needs Valium to settle her nerves on leaving our house, as the kids are so noisy. Well, we do have four of them.

In her opinion, I had my children too close together and questions why I didn't space them out like she did with hers. After she left my dad, she had another daughter, Louise, who is twelve years younger than me. Mum could only ever deal with one child at a time.

What I've learned from my mother is to embrace the positive attributes she has passed onto me and be mindful of the negative ones. I have her enquiring mind, thirst for knowledge, love of history and travel, and wicked sense of humour. She taught me the value of maintaining my individuality and independence, to never back away from a challenge, and to never be afraid to voice my opinions. She taught me that it's up to each of us to be the best person and parent we can be.

My mother had no parenting handbook. She did the best she could with what she knew, and it's not for me to judge her. She is the one who has to live with her life decisions.

4

Nursing

When I was seventeen, I started working at the local hospital. Initially I worked as an assistant in nursing, until I could gain entry to do my nurse's training. I have now been nursing for twenty-three years.

The first dead body I ever saw was old family friend who passed away that same year; little did I know then that it would the first of many.

I was once involved in resuscitating my grandfather, my dad's father. I was ill at home when I received a call from the hospital to say my grandfather had collapsed and the ambulance was out of town. I was collected in the back of the spare ambulance, with a police officer driving because there were no available Queensland Ambulance Service officers.

When the ambulance arrived at my grandfather's home I asked where the nurse was. They were short staffed and there was no nurse. As I was on the spot and a trained nurse, I was expected to accompany him to the hospital in the ambulance.

As we set off, the police officer asked how serious it was. I told him I'd started CPR, which I continued until we got there. I was comforted to see one of my trusted work colleagues waiting to help me when we arrived. It's a moment I will never forget.

Heartache touched me again when my cherished father died from cancer in 2000, and I also nursed my mother's mother at her home when she was dying of cancer. More recently, my best friend Jean's mother Fay also succumbed to cancer. Jean is one of my oldest friends, and is like a sister to me and an aunt to my children. I was also very close to Fay, who was like a second mother to me and an honorary grandmother to my children.

I think I was destined to become a nurse so I could be there to care for all these loved ones. Having grown up in a small town, I've witnessed so many old local characters passing onto the next life. I've cared for them and their loved ones to the best of my ability, drawing strength from my own experiences. At times nurses in small communities often have to care for friends, and even family members. This is especially hard when those people are dying. For such a small town, we lose quite a lot of residents of all ages to cancer.

In that time I have become a wife and a mother, with the gamut of emotions those roles involve. I am also a close friend, a niece, and a cousin, all of which has given me a wealth of knowledge of the ever-evolving cycle of life.

I went to a counsellor when I was twenty-four, for twelve months, and it was the most important thing I could have done for myself. One of the first things my counsellor congratulated me on was addressing my childhood issues and not letting them consume me.

Some people go their whole lives without confronting their issues, and because of this become bitter and twisted human beings. None of us can change what has taken place in our childhood, but we can change how we allow it to define the adult we want to become. I chose to develop mechanisms that allowed me to embrace life with love, and to give me the inner strength to handle life's obstacles.

For example, nursing can be a thankless and selfless profession. We spend our whole time caring for other people and very few people thank us for that concern and care. Perhaps it's because we give our all in being so caring and nurturing to our patients (well, good nurses do) that we have little tolerance for illness at home. My standard reply to someone sick at home is, 'Do you want some Panadol?'

It takes a lot to faze me, and unless someone has a broken bone, or blood pouring out of them, it's just a mere irritation to me, to my children's annoyance. They want me to look at every bump, scratch and cut on their body. Nine times out of ten it doesn't require much treatment, and a Band-Aid and kissing it better always makes it feel much better. Unfortunately that strategy doesn't work as well now they're getting older.

Unexpected dramas can and do unfold all the time and nurses tend to have a rather warped sense of humour. In reality it's probably a coping mechanism to help us deal with some of the harsher realities of life we're faced with on a daily basis. We can find laughter in the simplest things. If we're lucky enough to work with a good team of nurses, practical jokes can come fast and hard. I've shared many laughs with my colleagues over the years.

Nurses often have fond nicknames for their patients. A couple of brothers who were regular patients became known as 'Wallace and Grommet'. Another patient who always wore an ornate satin dressing gown became known as 'Prince Charming'.

I was once told a story about an operation where the female patient's pubic hair caught alight from the diathermy during surgery. The doctor very calmly said to the scrub nurse, 'Bushfire, bushfire.' She promptly used a wet sponge to extinguish the fire.

On another occasion, when I was working with a bitch of a nurse, we were cleaning a patient up after a 'code brown' (copious amounts of faeces). As we repositioned the patient to face the other side of the bed, a large amount of shit flicked up and landed strategically in the bitchy nurse's pocket. It couldn't have happened to a better person.

Over the years I've had faeces land in my shoes and on my leg, and have had urine squirted onto me by an elderly man whose old fella had shrivelled up to resemble a flower bud.

Nursing elderly patients often tends to give way to moments of hilarity; many an elderly person has had us in fits of laughter. Faeces is just one of those necessary evils in nursing, and all nurses, even the lazy ones, have to clean up it up at some stage.

One old lady who suffered from alcohol-induced dementia used the bedside screens as toilet paper. If we had to touch the screens in the room she shared, it was done at our own risk.

One of my favourite patients was a lovely lady, eighty-four years young, who came to live in town with her daughter when she was suffering from cancer. Her health deteriorated and she was admitted to hospital as a permanent patient. This lady of very advanced years had lacier bras than I had, with matching underpants. She had been a music teacher and loved listening to her music.

The very first day I had to shower her I asked if she was able to wash herself. She told me she could do 'wella, bella, and in between' as she pointed to her chest and nether regions. It was so cute.

When I tucked her into bed at night she loved to pat my face. She would rub her finger underneath my nose and call it 'velvet'. It was her favourite spot, she said. I would let her do it, thinking how cute she was, until one night when I wondered what I could smell. I looked at her hand and there it was—faeces jam-packed under her fingernails. Needless to say, from that day on I was very careful to ensure her hands and nails were spotless before she stroked my velvet.

One evening shift I was working with another close friend when one of our regular alcoholics came in. Unfortunately, this time he was DOA, which was a shame as he was such a colourful character. We went over to the morgue to grab the trolley. When we got it back to the ward my friend thought I had put the brakes on and I thought she had. We had the trolley pushed up against the ward bed ready to transfer the body to the morgue trolley completely unaware that the brakes weren't engaged.

It was like something out of *Mr Bean*. The trolley started moving away from us in slow motion, and even though this man wasn't large, he was still heavy and he ended up on the floor. Thankfully he had a tough skull. That had been made evident on a previous admission, when he had fallen headfirst into the toilet in his drunken state and totally smashed the toilet cistern, sustaining only a scratch to his head.

So we were pretty confident there would be no head fractures, but we were then faced with the dilemma of how we were going to lift this body up off the floor, in between fits of giggles, and put him back on the trolley.

Nursing has blessed me with some of my closest friends and has also given me some of the wackiest and funniest memories in my life thus far.

I recall a very disagreeable patient we had in hospital who never wanted to come inside at bedtime. She would sit outside on the veranda, chain-smoking. The nurse in charge and I devised a plan to go outside, hide behind a tree, ring a bell and hopefully the patient would think there was someone out there and get herself inside.

It backfired on us slightly. She sat staring in the direction of the bell, and we were stuck outside hiding behind a tree. Thankfully the other nurse on duty came to our rescue. She told the woman that the police had phoned with reports of prowlers in the area. Needless to say, the woman promptly stopped her smoking and arguing with the staff and scuttled inside, and we were able to come out of hiding and get back to our posts in the hospital.

The security at the hospital is much better now, but years ago my friend and I were on night duty together when a less-than-charming drunk guy came in to be stitched up after a fight. As he left, full of booze and bad manners, he decided to tear the glass front door clean off one hinge. We were very resourceful and tied it back against the railing with autoclaving tape, which meant we spent the rest of the night shift with the front entry door wide open.

My mother worked at the same hospital for nearly twenty years and has some of the funniest nursing stories I have ever heard. Sometimes I sit down to reminisce with her colleagues of that era and walk away with a sore jaw from laughing so hard. Their stories are priceless.

I was a hospital-trained enrolled nurse. After my dad died, I did a university degree and became a registered nurse. My first night shift as an enrolled nurse was a real eye-opener, as the night sister who worked the weekend shift, 'Nurse Nightingale', was a law unto herself. Whichever enrolled nurse was rostered to work with her was instructed to collect Nurse Nightingale, who didn't drive, from her home on their way to the hospital.

One night that duty fell to me. She got in the car and immediately started gossiping and criticising every nurse on the roster, starting at the top of the list and clearly set on working her way through them all. She didn't get very far, as I quickly informed her I wasn't interested, so she switched to running down the remaining residents of the town. She spent the majority of every shift sitting in her chair doing cross-stitch, while whoever worked with her ran around and did all the work.

I was taught the routine of night duty by the best; namely, work as much as possible to a set routine at the start of a shift. The ward servery had to be spic and span, with the electric urns topped up and set to boil. The soiled-linen bags were tied off and replaced every night, and loaded into the linen trolley to be removed by the wardsperson the next morning.

We tidied the pan room, and scrubbed the sinks and benches until we could almost see our faces in the stainless steel. Any containers with Milton solutions and the lotion the mercury thermometers soaked in were changed at midnight. The trollies were loaded with whatever we'd need for the overnight rounds and then we were ready for whatever the shift might throw at us.

Whenever a popular staff member resigned, it was tradition for them to be dunked in the big enamel bathtub we used to have on the ward. It would be filled with a revolting concoction of oils and other yucky stuff, and then baby powder would be puffed all over them. Rather like a modern-day tarring and feathering. If they didn't get dunked in that tub on their last shift, they knew they weren't going to be missed.

One of my best friends was acting director of nursing for over seven months, and it was the best fun we had at that hospital in years. She and a fellow wardsperson organised to jack my little Mitsubishi Colt up off its wheels. When I finished work and went to drive off, the wheels just spun around. I couldn't believe I hadn't noticed that 'Camilla' was sitting up a little higher than usual

What I've learned during my years of nursing is to appreciate the value of every day, not to be judgemental of others, and to trust in the skills of my colleagues. I can't change how other people behave, but I have the power to change how I react and respond to other people's actions. It's rewarding to be a part of a skilled team that treats the diversity of problems challenging the patients. To witness the dignity and courage with which they cope is very humbling.

5

Travel

At the age of twenty-four, I took eleven months and three weeks unpaid leave from work. My best friend Jean and I flew from Brisbane to Sydney and on to the United States, starting our adventure in Los Angeles.

Jean stayed with me for about seven weeks during the North American part of the trip. She's a mixture of European, Chinese and Aborigine, which means she often finds herself being classified as any one of a number of races. On arrival at LAX, we were held up as they thought she was a Mexican trying to come into the country on an Australian passport.

That was just the first of several such encounters. I wish I had a dollar for every time someone addressed her in Spanish when we were in Mexico. It could have bought us a few tequilas.

While waiting at a bus stop in Billings, Montana, a lovely Native American came over and asked Jean what tribe she was from. Jean loves Native American Indians so that made her year.

Even in Australia, people often think she's of Maori descent. 'Which island, North or South?' they ask. Her usual response is, 'Australia.'

In Los Angeles we did the usual touristy things, including Disneyland and Universal Studios. Then we went to San Francisco via Amtrak Rail, where Jean lost her luggage for two days.

A few days later we travelled to Seattle and went on a Canadian Contiki tour. OMG. What an experience that was. Because we didn't bonk anyone and totally write ourselves off every night of the week with grog, the group ostracised us a bit. Thankfully we made friends with two nice guys from country New South Wales who weren't there to fornicate their way around Canada either.

Eventually we arrived in Calgary, which was the main reason we did the tour—to go to the Calgary Stampede. I had a migraine kicking in, so I was grateful when we arrived at the hotel and could finally lie down. Later that night we went out for dinner, and my defence of the episode I'm about to relate is that I was still a bit doughy from the Aspalgin I'd taken for my headache.

I needed to use the toilet, and when I use a public toilet I always put toilet paper on the seat. After I left the facilities, I wondered why people were looking at me but didn't think too much of it.

We finished dinner and got up to leave, with Jean walking in front of me to pay for our meal. She turned around as I walked out the door and there it was—a long trail of toilet paper hanging out of the back of my jeans. Total humiliation. Thank god YouTube or Facebook didn't exist back then.

Jean couldn't stop laughing, while I just wanted the ground to open up and swallow me. I was so grateful to be in another country where I would never see those people again.

The Calgary Stampede was brilliant. We were travelling on a budget so we didn't want to waste our money on alcohol, but they were selling huge plastic cups filled with icy cold Budweiser for four dollars. We took advantage of that bargain, which led to my next embarrassing moment in Calgary. I walked into the men's toilet by mistake. I saw guys walking past me, but in my Budweiser haze I didn't twig to the situation until I was fully inside. We slowed down on the bargain Budweisers after that.

On the way back to Vancouver, where the tour ended, we went to a male strip show in Kamloops. That was a *real* eye-opener. Jean and I had just told a couple of German girls, who were also on the tour, that in Australia male strippers just dance and only strip down to their jocks. We were in for a shock; these strippers did the full monty. The German girls' mouths were hanging open, too. They were glued to the spot, unable to move, clapping their hands madly.

Then the comments started:

'Oh yeah, that's big.'

'Ohmygod, you could beat someone to death with that and then use it as towel rack.'

The stripper in question was from Barbados and I'm pretty damn sure that one would bring tears to the eyes.

5 TRAVEL

In Vancouver we did a boat trip, went to the Hard Rock Cafe and met up with everyone from the tour at a bar. Rob, the bus driver, introduced us to his gorgeous girlfriend. Unbeknown to her, he had been shagging all the available girls on the tour. He had been like a child in a candy store. Mmm, which one will I have tonight?

We shared a hire car with another couple and drove back to Seattle for the next stage of our trip, when we travelled through the United States by bus. From Seattle we went to Cody, Wyoming for a couple of days, and then onto Flagstaff, Arizona.

At one point in our bus travel, Jean and I couldn't get seats together. I ended up sitting next to a guy who had just got out of prison for drug trafficking and was on a one-way ticket home. He was full of chatter and shared his life history. He had taken a shine to me and wanted to be penpals, so I gave him a dodgy address and a false name. Next thing I know I'd ended up with a friendship bracelet. The whole thing freaked me out.

We arrived in Flagstaff at midnight and caught a taxi to the hostel. By that time we were exhausted. Our taxi driver looked like a neo-Nazi. Another guy was bugging us at the terminal. It's safe to say that we two country girls, who had never travelled overseas before, were pretty keen to reach the safety of our room.

The next day we saw the Grand Canyon, which was beyond amazing. Then we went to Phoenix and Houston before leaving for Mexico City. What a trip it had been so far.

On our first day in Mexico City we went on a tour to Chapultepec Castle, where I was felt up by the most unattractive man. I couldn't believe it. I was wearing homemade board shorts, T-shirt, cap and sneakers. There was nothing appealing or sexy about me, so why, out of all the women around, did he have to pick *me*? He put his hand between my legs from behind and groped my genitals. There were a couple of French women on the tour who were getting around in singlet tops and shorts that just covered their butt, with their long blonde hair cascading around them and strutting their stuff, inviting someone to maul them. But no, it was the daggy-looking Australian chick that tickled his fancy.

I was thrilled when we left Mexico City. Our next stop was Taxco, which was full of silver shops. It should have taken us thirty minutes to walk to our hotel, but it took us two and a half hours. I'm sure we went in nearly every store. The custom in Mexico is to barter. I didn't master it very well, but Jean did. She got the same look on her face that her father gets when he's about to fight someone. She came across as very intimidating, and we were able to buy some beautiful pieces.

I loved Acapulco. One evening we went to dinner where a jug with a funnel-type spout was passed around. The trick was to drink from it while someone slowly poured the liquid into your mouth. There were only four people who could finish it—three guys from Australia and me, which says a lot about Australians.

I drank some orange juice, and in my wisdom didn't even think it might have been reconstituted with local tap water. I got the worst case of diarrhoea. I shit for nearly a week. I had to keep taking Lomotil tablets to block me up just to be able to travel on the bus. Had I been in Australia, I would have been on an intravenous drip. This whole bowel experience

5 TRAVEL

gave me a lifelong friend called Polly. Yes, I named my pile.

I have two things to thank Mexico for. First was the tequila, and the second was Polly.

From Mexico we made a little detour to El Paso, Texas. We're both avid John Wayne fans, so we had to have a look at where one of his movies was set.

Our next port of call was New Orleans and I have to say it was by far my favourite city in the United States. We both loved it. I'm a huge fan of the movie *Gone with the Wind*, so we took a tour to Oak Alley plantation (in the movie it was known fondly as Twelve Oaks). We couldn't go inside as John Travolta was on location, filming a movie called *Primary Colours*.

In New Orleans we ate the best food of our entire time in the States—gumbo and jambalaya. I felt I had died and gone to heaven, and it was a heaven called New Orleans. We also loved hearing about the scandalous past of Laura Plantation, where the story of Brer Rabbit and the Tar Baby was set.

We travelled by train from New Orleans to New York, and when we arrived at Penn Station a man came up, grabbed our luggage and rushed off with it. All we could do was follow him, yelling at him to give it back, which he did once we got to the subway. He insisted we buy two tokens and tried to make Jean pay him $11.50. She gave him a five and a ten. Well, the rest is history. He ran. He obviously saw us coming. At least we got our luggage back.

We did the usual touristy things in New York and after three nights Jean flew back to Australia. It was amazing sharing the North American leg of my journey with her.

We had a lot of fun and it was good to be with someone I was close to, to help me get over my homesickness.

On the next leg of my trip I stayed with Glennis, a lovely person who had worked as a nanny on my grandma's property years before and they had kept in touch. I travelled by bus from New York to her home on the outskirts of Nappanee in Canada. I spent nearly two weeks with her, and in that time we went travelling together. We stayed in Burlington, Canada for one night, and then went on to Calais in Maine, and finally to Prince Edward Island, where we visited the *Anne of Green Gables* locations as well as saw the *Anne of Green Gables* musical.

Next I stayed with the parents of a Canadian girl I had worked at the hospital with years before. They were very kind and generous to me. The day before I was due to leave for London, Anne, my friend's mother, got a call from Juliet, a friend in Toronto, who was looking for a nanny to look after her children when they went on holiday. Anne told Juliet she had the perfect young lady to fill that role, but unfortunately I was leaving the next day for London.

While in London I received a call from Juliet, answered a few simple questions, and three weeks later I was on a plane to Toronto, all expenses paid, to accompany her and her two daughters on holiday to Hilton Head Island in South Carolina.

That was the start of my time with Juliet and her daughters. The two girls were gorgeous. They were four and three, and would be grown women today, possibly with children of their own. One of the cutest moments was at the beach when the youngest girl asked a man if he stole little girls. When he said he didn't, she turned around and shouted to her mum, 'It's okay, he doesn't steal little girls.'

After Canada, I went back to London and travelled through Europe by Eurobus with Gemma, an Australian mate from home. One of our stops was the Czech Republic. While there I got a taste for cheap red supermarket wine. We also decided to try a drink called absinthe. First you light up a spoonful of sugar, wait for the flames to go out, stir it into the green liquid and down the hatch it goes. Absinthe used to be illegal everywhere except Spain, and for good reason, as it's renowned for sending people mad.

After having one drink I went for a shower and thought I was on the set of *Psycho*. Gemma decided that sleeping outside in the fresh air was something she wanted to do (basically she went mad and decided she was going to hitchhike back to Queensland), and another girl went into an absinthe-induced coma.

I'm pretty straight when it comes to drugs, so imagine my horror when, in a moment of weakness, I ended up in a compromising situation in Amsterdam. I'll blame the weather, as it had been raining all day and someone suggested that four of us go to a coffee shop. Off we trotted, thinking we were clever and daring. We found a coffee shop and didn't pay much attention to our surroundings at first. Then someone suggested we should have gone somewhere else.

I looked around and saw a couple of guys straight out of Village People getting awfully cosy together. One of our guys was feeling uncomfortable, but we decided that as we were already there we should buy something. We bought a slice of the 'special' cake and broke it into four pieces. It may have tasted like Madeira cake but it had more in it than just the basic eggs, sugar and flour.

We headed back to the hostel for happy hour and then it hit us. I became paranoid and thought people were talking about me. Gemma depleted the snack-vending machine of food. One of the guys admired the architecture and became a professional in a split second. By six pm I had to be put to bed. I couldn't function and I couldn't snap out of it. I lay in bed crying, and then felt strangely calm and relaxed and really weird.

Needless to say, I've never done anything like that again. The only drugs since are those that can be bought over the counter from a chemist and will fix a headache.

I was so used to telling my dad everything that I sent him a postcard telling him I got high in Amsterdam. I don't know what possessed me to write and tell him. It's not like it was an escapade in my hometown that the local barmaid would be able to spread around town. I was on the other side of the world and he wasn't likely to find out about it. True to form, no judgements were ever passed by him.

Gemma and I went to the opera in Vienna and then it was on to Rome.

Rome was amazing. We visited all the tourist sights and stayed in dodgy hostels. One room had fourteen bunk beds crammed into it. The guy who ran the hostel thought he was Don Juan DeMarco and kept flashing his sexy body (not) to us. In reality he looked like an Italian beach ball. On our second night there he decided to throw his fat gut around, and picked on a long-haired Swiss guy, a psychology major, who calmly talked his way through the conflict. Beach Ball became irrational and tried to ring the police, to no avail. Then he announced he was going to phone his Turkish henchmen.

Later, when we were tucked up in bed, Gemma and I laughed so hard at Beach Ball's shenanigans.

One morning at about five am Gemma and I had two intruders in our room that just about scared the shit clean out of us. They were two Italian guys, dressed in leather. When I shined my torch on them, they closed the door and we could hear a hell of a racket in the common room. We didn't sleep too well after that.

After seeing the movie *Taken*, I sometimes think how lucky we were in Rome while staying at that dodgy hostel. I think we were lucky to leave Rome in one piece.

After Rome I travelled with a group of friends Nice, and then we did a day trip to Monaco. I enjoyed both cities, and being an avid Grace Kelly fan, Monaco was a highlight. My time in Europe came to an end via Lucerne, Basel, Barcelona, Madrid, San Sebastian and Paris.

Then it was back to London for Christmas and New Year's. I went to a party at the home of one of my cousin's rugby mates. OMG. What a night. I got drunk, my cousin's wife decided she wasn't talking to me anymore, another couple got into an argument, an ageing rugby hooker and a middle-aged Scotsman chatted me up, and then we all trooped out to the front yard to watch the fireworks.

Much to my disgust, I had to ride in the boot on the way home. What a way to see in 1998: drunk and being transported in a car boot, calling for somebody to let me out.

After London, I headed to Scotland and met up with a close friend from home, Maree, who was also a nurse, and her boyfriend Dick. Maree's employer had set her up with a three-room flat. I signed on with the same agency and ended up nursing in Aberdeen for two months.

Aberdeen was a real adventure. Not only did our town in Queensland have no traffic lights, but there was no public transport either, so catching buses to and from work in Aberdeen was an experience. I remember waiting at the bus stop one night when it started to snow. Wow, that took the whole catching-a-bus-to-work-experience to another level. I was used to getting in my car and being four minutes max from home, and now here was the country girl catching, on some days, two different buses to get home.

The nursing system in Scotland was different to what I was used to, and I couldn't believe how dismal the wages were. I met many interesting characters in hospital, and I also had the humbling experience of working in a head-injury ward for over a week. After working one shift there, I must have impressed someone as the agency was soon phoning to say the ward had requested me to go back for ten days.

I had mixed emotions working on that ward. At times I was profoundly saddened by a patient's prognosis, and then elated when someone did something as simple as move their hand or took their first step.

One patient who really affected me was a young man around my age who had gone out partying after his twenty-first birthday celebrations at home. He was beaten up by bouncers at a pub, and after that the only part of him that worked were his eyes. He couldn't move, or speak, but he could cry. Some days he was so sad that tears would just roll down his cheeks. They believed his mind was still working and he understood everything going on around him. He loved the radio, and on the days he was happy his beautiful eyes shone.

After Aberdeen I went back to Holland and stayed with family friends. Then I went to Ireland with my cousin's sister-in-law, Linda. We stayed with her relatives, which was a great way to experience Ireland. My only problem on that trip was when Linda decided to give up smoking.

We stayed with Linda's uncle and aunt in Dublin, and on our first night out Linda smoked a straw. She told me that non-smokers were boring and began criticising anyone who didn't smoke. I didn't—and don't—smoke, and here I was out with a newly minted non-smoker who was like a bear with a sore head. After I had drunk my first Kilkenny and many more drinks, we staggered to our bus and arrived safely home to find Linda's uncle and aunt waiting up for us to have a nightcap. Linda was too far gone, but the drunken Aussie had a scotch.

The next day we drove to the home of another of Linda's aunts, an ex-nurse who lived on a farm and made the most incredible soda bread, and rhubarb crumble with homemade pastry. We visited Linda's mother's hometown of Creggs, and stayed with a cousin in Galway who was a 'white witch.' Linda was taking a trip down memory lane and it was lovely sharing it with her.

The next day we went with a few people to a 'signature tree'. We stood and watched as they walked around the tree, meditating and talking to the tree to reenergise themselves. I now have a much broader outlook on most alternative therapies, but at the time I thought it was pretty funny.

After our experience of tree talking, we hit the pubs on St Paddy's Day. Moments later I was chatting to a guy who was friends with a man whose kids I used to babysit at home. I couldn't believe it. We celebrated in true Irish style.

Linda was pretty drunk by that stage. Instead of waiting to catch a taxi, she insisted I drive her car home, which was not one of my smartest decisions. She vomited once on the way home and then another time when we got home. I parked the car—in someone else's driveway. The next morning when we came out the car was gone, the only evidence it had been there Linda's dried-up vomit. Into the nearest police station we went, to be told they had impounded the missing car. The neighbour had called the police when they couldn't get out for work. After much pleading, we got our car back and had to pay a sixty-pound fine.

Our next port of call was a cousin's house in Cork. OMG, our bedroom was like a hotel room. We had our own TV and DVD player. For this tired backpacker, it felt like heaven.

My time in Ireland was amazing. Even if I go back again it will never be the same as spending it with Linda and her very welcoming family, all totally different but also totally the same in the warmth they extend to people. My time in the UK had come to an end.

I flew to Paris and met up with Maree again. We stayed there for a week in a pension, living on

Camembert, baguettes and red wine. One night we treated ourselves to a restaurant meal and I tried escargot. It doesn't matter how exotic the name seems, at the end of the day it's just a snail.

After Paris, Maree flew back to England and I went to Africa.

My plane landed in Harare, and began my African trip with a close call. Instead of dropping me at a backpackers' hostel, the driver took me to a halfway house. Luckily for me, a lady had just delivered a troubled man there from her congregation in church. She pulled me aside and said, 'This isn't the place for you. I run a travel agency in town. If you want to come with me I can help you.'

She helped me find accommodation and organise my train and bus fares to Victoria Falls, where I was to connect with my tour. The train was so old-world that everything was timber. At night a man came around and turned down my bed, reminding me of the book *The Power of One*. I was advised to tie my backpack to the bedrail and up by my head. When the train pulled up at smaller stations through the night, it was explained, people would look in the windows and if they saw unguarded possessions they would think all their Christmases had come at once.

I found Africa a safe place to travel, and the people were very helpful and friendly. Our tour only went to the safer parts , so I soon began to feel confident that I would survive this adventure. My four weeks in Africa were amazing and I met some wonderful people. Except for two people, everyone else was Australian.

Seeing my first elephant in the wild was mind-blowing. The markets were incredible, and the people so clever with their crafts. Having an icy cold coke on the veranda of the Victoria Falls Hotel was awesome, as it's a beautiful establishment. All I could afford was a Coke, but I promised myself there and then that if I ever came back to Africa I would stay at the Victoria Falls Hotel (which I did, but more about that later).

To this day, my husband James finds it amazing that I slept in a tent for four weeks in Africa when he can't even get me to go camping at home. But my days of backpacking are well and truly over. Gone are the days of sharing a room with a minimum of ten people, inhaling their body odour, foot odour and gas. I loved the experience of backpacking for twelve months, but I think we all evolve and mature, and the days of sharing a communal bathroom are long gone. I don't miss eating out of a beer stein either.

I was a small-town country girl entering the big wide world to see what life had to offer, and I experienced things I had never even dreamed of.

What I've learned about travelling is to be receptive to change. Everyone has their unique story to share, and sometimes these stories and shared experiences help us see life from an entirely different perspective, which can be truly inspiring. I always tried to greet people in their own language; I tried new cuisines and revelled in the different cultures. I met people from all walks of life, including white witches in Ireland, and I nursed head-injury victims in Scotland. I was privileged to see how other people live, and I embraced the experience with an open mind and heart.

The Proposal

In 2000, before James and I were married, I was invited to attend a friend's wedding in England. James came with me to Africa, where we stayed for ten days before he flew back to Australia and I carried on to England. We took James's mother Betty with us. Now *that* was an experience. Betty had never flown before. She became dehydrated on the plane so James had to keep asking the flight attendant for water. Then she started burping with bad indigestion from a Chinese meal that she had eaten two days before. She sounded like a bullfrog during mating season.

When we arrived at Victoria Falls I was feeling quite romantic. We had spent the night in Johannesburg, where James and I had gone shopping at Rand Mall and unintentionally bought a diamond. It was a lot of fun. Following that we had walked around and looked at different styles of engagement rings, to see what I liked. It was the most fun we had ever had shopping together. Obviously I was half expecting a proposal, especially since I had kept my promise to myself from a couple of years before and our next stop was the Victoria Falls Hotel.

I had booked a king-sized room for James and me. I didn't tell him how much the room cost per night but it was close to a week's wage. I had explained to Betty that the hotel wasn't cheap and asked if she would prefer to stay elsewhere. She said she wouldn't.

We checked in and discovered that Betty, who was at the other end of the hotel, was not happy. At this point she had a face on her like a bashed-in jam tin. So stupid here asked the staff if there was a spare room near hers we could be shifted to. That was soon arranged. No problem. That is, until I opened the door to our new room and saw two single beds. Not only did we forgo the king-sized bed in our original room, we didn't even get to sleep in the same bed.

I remained calm and suggested we go to the Livingstone Restaurant for dinner, hoping it would set the mood for a proposal. How romantic it would be for James to propose at the Victoria Falls Hotel, I thought.

At the restaurant James had to wear a suit jacket, which they supplied. We had a lovely five-course meal. The only hiccup was that Betty came with us. I can still hear the band singing Louis Armstrong's song 'What a Wonderful World.' It was quite surreal, but there was no proposal that night.

The next day before going to the markets we went to Betty's room and couldn't believe our eyes. She had

6 THE PROPOSAL

brought nearly ten kilos of coins with her as spending money. It suddenly made sense why she kept getting charged for excess baggage. It wouldn't have helped that she was also carrying a coffee mug that could hold about one litre of tea or coffee, which, much to our embarrassment, she would produce every morning and ask the wait staff to fill.

She bartered so vigorously with one guy at the markets I had visions of a machete striking her any minute.

The next part of our journey took us to Etosha National Park. We hired a car and drove around for nearly four days. After leaving Windhoek we caught a bus to Cape Town. Still no proposal.

During our travels, if there were only two seats available side by side, James would sit with his mum and I would sit by myself. On this day James told his mum he was sitting beside me, so she put a bag on the spare seat next to her. Trust me, she has a look that would deter anyone from sitting next to her.

James sat down beside me on the bus and the proposal finally happened. His words were: 'So, how about it? Do you wanna get married?'

Just like that. Where was the romance? No proposal during a romantic dinner at the Victoria Falls Hotel. No proposal while watching the falls from the hotel. Instead, it happened while we travelled on a bus from Windhoek to Cape Town.

I said yes. What was I thinking? The next words out of his mouth were, 'How about a head job?' Needless to say, that didn't happen, with his mother a few seats behind us.

That was my marriage proposal. No hearts, no flowers or candles, nothing that vaguely resembled romance.

What I've learned about proposals is not to set your hopes too high and that way you won't be disappointed. Keep your expectations to a minimum, and also think twice before taking family members along on holiday, especially when expecting the traditional hearts-and-flowers wedding proposal.

7

The Wedding

After his romantic proposal, James and his mother travelled back to Australia. I went to the wedding in England, and then visited friends in Canada. While in Canada I found my wedding dress. I'd been dreading the day I would have to choose a wedding dress. As everyone travelling overseas with me knows, I deliberate over what postcards to buy and who will receive which postcard, so choosing something as important as a wedding dress was always going to be a nightmare.

However, nothing could have been further from the truth. It was most likely the easiest thing I have chosen in my life. I was hanging out with Ann's daughter, and she told me about an amazing bridal shop. They asked my preferred price range and only showed me the gowns in that range. There was no drooling over dresses that were totally out of my price range.

I was handed a form to fill in, and one of the questions was: *What style are you looking for?* The only thing I could think of was something between Grace Kelly and Audrey Hepburn. I love simple but elegant. We were taken into a room and shown a dress that I thought was a bit plain, but then I tried it on and it was stunning. I just loved it.

Before making a final decision, however, I had to go back a second time so Anne, my Canadian friend, could see me in it. She was speechless and tears ran down her cheeks. Now, *that* was the impact I wanted to make. I was fortunate that it fit me beautifully, and cost me only eight hundred dollars as it was off the rack.

I phoned Australia to tell Aunty Bella about my wedding dress. It was an emotional moment for me, as my dad had always said that with him being a single parent he would never be able to afford to pay for my wedding, although he would pay for my wedding dress. But my dad was gone.

So the deal was done. I paid a deposit and would pay off the rest. Anne would bring it to Australia when she came for the wedding.

On my arrival back in Australia, Aunty Bella came out to see me at the airport. Before I caught my connecting flight home she shoved an envelope in my pocket and said not to open it until I was on the plane. I had an inkling of what it was and I was correct. There in the envelope were eight hundred dollars and a note saying, *From your dad*. I was in floods of tears. I was so moved by her generous gesture. I promptly paid off my dress.

No one ever really tells us how stressful organising a wedding is. Some people will admit some stress and others no stress. Well, I can say James and I nearly called the wedding off after disagreeing about the wedding cake. How stupid is that? Finding someone

7 THE WEDDING

to make my cake that actually lived closer than eight hundred kilometres away caused the stress meter to go up a lot. In the end I found a lady in Townsville who was able to make what we wanted, and another good friend was able to bring it on the plane with her.

James had no real input into the wedding and nor did he want to, so with amazing help from my closest friends and Aunty Bella we eventually got to the day without too many more explosions.

My father had passed the year before and my mother wasn't into weddings, but I was fortunate to have amazing support from friends and family. One of my friends made the bridesmaids' dresses and did an incredible job, and she also printed the wedding invitations. All my closest friends had a role to play. If one friend wasn't a bridesmaid, she did a reading instead.

My family also had roles to play. One cousin was on tour with the arts council, but my uncle organised her travel arrangements so she could make it to the wedding to play the organ. I left the church music in her capable hands, and she chose and played gorgeous music. Another cousin videotaped the service, and yet another did a reading. My uncles and aunties, plus my dad's first cousins, who I refer to as uncle and aunty, also pitched in and set up the reception area.

I would love to have been a fly on the wall while that was happening, as I have very strong women in my family and none of them take kindly to being told what to do. I had some feedback from the younger generation, but I'm still not sure who took on the role of queen bee boss. There would have been some interesting family dynamics afoot.

I'M FORTY

Aunty Bella, my dad's adored youngest sister, spoke on his behalf at our wedding. Anyone else important drove bridal cars. I involved my family as much as possible in my wedding. We were raised to be family orientated and it's only since we've grown up and drifted apart that some of that extended family closeness is waning.

I couldn't choose anyone to give me away, as I couldn't replace my father, so I bucked tradition and had James come from the front of the church and walk me down the aisle.

When asked, 'Who gives this woman to this man?' I promptly replied, 'My father.' I was told later that there were not many dry eyes in the church.

I didn't experience any nerves on the day and I was quite calm walking up the aisle, so that must have been a good sign. I didn't get to view this firsthand but someone had adorned James's shoes with the words *Help me* on their soles. The photographer took a photo of that for me.

My mother was unable to attend my wedding, but her eighty-four-year-old mother represented that side of the family. She travelled thirteen hundred kilometres to attend, and said she would not have missed it. Interestingly enough, Grandma had not attended any of her own daughters' or sons' weddings, for various reasons. Ours was the only family wedding she ever attended, apart from my older male cousin's.

Our wedding reception was held at the local racecourse and it turned into an all-nighter. At five am, there were just five of us still standing. We went home just on daylight and were back at eight-thirty am to start the recovery breakfast. We had a lamb on a spit and the celebrations continued. The racecourse was the perfect venue for our reception

7 THE WEDDING

because we didn't have to concern ourselves about noise control, and we had a live band playing until two am.

The hen night was held two nights before the wedding. A bus was organised and a friend drove us to a nearby town. I'm not sure if many people can say their future husband came to their house to help them get organised for their hen night, helping to attach condoms to their hen-night veil.

My dear friend, who did all the sewing and printing preparations for the hen night, was so exhausted she took a raincheck and stayed at home to recuperate for the big day. Mind you, she made up for it at the wedding.

James and I paid for our wedding. His parents contributed towards the alcohol but we paid the rest. James even cashed in one of his life insurance policies to help with the cost. The only concern I had—and we all have one after a wedding when we start psychoanalysing the night—was that the lighting could have been better. There weren't enough candles, and for a while during the meal it was very dark until someone turned on the big fluorescent lights. It ruined the ambience I was trying to create, but after all these years, who cares about the lighting, and does anyone else remember anyway?

At midnight I developed a migraine, so a few nurses went to the hospital and grabbed some Aspalgin tablets for me. I took those, rested in someone's car, and woke up about one am. The night was still young.

When James and I did go back to our flat, one of the bridesmaids and her partner were in our bed, so we pulled out the sofa bed and slept on that for a few hours.

I didn't have to organise everything. I had read somewhere that the groom-to-be organises the honeymoon, so I gave him free rein with that and he did a brilliant job, after asking the older men he worked with for ideas. Mind you, he went through three travel agents before he found one that he felt comfortable talking to.

When I asked him if I needed my passport, all he would say was, 'Pack it, just in case.'

I didn't know where we were going until the morning of our flight. I figured it had to be overseas when the taxi took us to the international airport. So off to Malaysia we went.

I still didn't know the final destination until we arrived at Kuala Lumpur airport and James said, 'Okay, I'll need your help now.' We had to catch a connecting flight to Langkwai Island.

We had an amazing time away and it was the best surprise.

At the end of the day, you can tick as many checklists as you like, but there will always be something you can nick-pick about, or find fault with. It's human nature. What I learned from my wedding day was to have fun and enjoy the day (or night). It's always about the bride, and it's always about staying and partying with your guests until the last one drops. Many of the guests travelled such a long way to share the celebration and I wanted to party with them at every moment. We made the decision to be the last ones to leave and we were.

What I've learned about weddings is that consummating the marriage on the bridal night is overrated. You have the rest of your life for that, so make the most of your wedding and enjoy.

8

My Husband

Husbands. OMG. I went to Melbourne for four days to buy stock at a gift fair for my shop. As always, a lot of work was involved before I could go away, even for four nights. I packed clothes for four kids and myself, fed the animals, washed the car, fuelled it and packed it, and cooked dinner. All James had to do was pack his own clothes. He was taking the kids to his parents' place in Charters Towers, and I would catch a flight from Townsville to Melbourne.

While I was fuelling the car James came home from work and rushed everyone out the door. I didn't check to see whether he had packed a bag. After a seven-hour drive, he arrived in Charters Towers in the early hours of Friday morning.

I flew to Melbourne that night and checked into my room. I got a phone call from James.

'Where did you put my bag?' he asked.

'What bag?'

'I can't find the bag with my clothes in it,' he said.

I felt bad for a fleeting moment, but then remembered *why* I hadn't packed one. I no longer do it for him, ever since he complained that I'd packed the wrong clothes. So there he was, stuck at his parents' place for three days with only the clothes on his back. After saying he was going for a shower, he promptly hung up on me.

OMG. Do I expect him to pack *my* clothes? No. To top it off, Thomas had gone through James's wallet three days before we left home. I kept asking him where Daddy's cards from his wallet were. He said they were in the 'big, big bin'. *I* went outside—not James—and searched for the cards. The rubbish truck empties the bin on Monday. I think Thomas may have committed this offence on Monday morning, because he kept saying 'the big, big truck came and took them'.

James had intended to cancel his cards the next day, when he arrived at Charters Towers.

Then I got a call from James asking if I remembered to put his wallet in the car before I left. *His* wallet, not my wallet, did I remember *his* wallet? No, I didn't. James was now stuck in Charters Towers with *no* clothes, *no* wallet, no identification and no money.

Why do men ask us where their things are? *Their* wallet, *their* phone, *their* hat, *their* sunglasses. Where is … where are … these are constant refrains. I use none of James's things. Does he hear me asking him to find *my* wallet, *my* phone? No. I know where my things are, and why would I expect James to know where they are anyway? He doesn't use them.

James can walk past his phone on the kitchen bench, go to bed, and then call out from the bedroom for someone to take his phone down to him. Most times he can con one of the four kids into doing it. He's lucky we have four kids so he can spread his laziness between them.

Don't get me wrong; I love my husband. James is my best male friend and when he isn't being picky and grouchy I enjoy his company. He works hard, provides for his family and loves working in his garden, but as for helping with domestic chores, or doing anything inside the house, I may as well beat my head against a brick wall.

For example, James will eat an apple while watching TV, put the core on the coffee table and get up and go back to the kitchen for something else. Does he grab that apple core? Oh, no.

Years ago when he did this I tried leaving it sitting there. No, I thought, I'm not picking that up and putting it in the bin. He can do that much. Well, that apple core sat there and sat there and sat there. Weeks later I finally gave in, when it was so dry and shrivelled I could barely recognise it for what it was.

I had tried and failed, and now I think that with all the things in life there are to worry about, that apple core is pretty insignificant.

As another example, I always love the times when he'll walk inside and say, 'The kids have taken your good saucepan outside.'

Does he pick it up? Oh, no. He leaves it for me to go outside and pick it up. Why? *Why,* when he's seen it, and walked past it, can't *he* pick it up?

On another occasion I was in the bedroom, cleaning and putting clothes away. I wasn't resting, meditating or doing anything for me. He walked all the way down to the bedroom to tell me Thomas had spilt milk all over the floor. Did he clean it up? No, he did not. But he felt the need to tell me. He must have thought I'd like the honour of cleaning it up.

He then wonders why I get annoyed. And why I watch shows like *Grey's Anatomy* and *Downton Abbey*. It's for some escapism from the reality of my wonderful lot.

I mentioned before that James is my best *male* friend. That's because I have some amazing close female friends. I've always treasured my female friendships, and there are things that I can share with them that I could never discuss with my husband.

I was talking to a friend recently who gave me a classic example of a typical husband's behaviour. She was upstairs ironing, and was also flat out getting the kids ready for school, pretty much a typical mother's morning. Her husband was downstairs feeding their puppies. The next thing he was singing out to her that one of the puppies had peed on the floor.

'What are you going to do about it?' she called back.

'I'm too busy,' he said. 'I don't have time to clean it up. I've got to go.'

Really. What goes through a male's brain at times like this? He was right there, but could he clean up the wee? No.

This lack of thought from our male counterparts is just mind-blowing. If we didn't laugh we would cry. This is why we need our girl talk—to get it off our chests. Otherwise we would go insane.

One of the things we discuss is our husbands' lack of support with homework. If they get home from work early, do they even think to help the kids with their homework? No. One friend told me she asked her husband to help one of their kids with her reading. All he did was tell his daughter she had to read the book. Then he went and sat himself down in front of the TV.

I can do one better. One day I sent our daughter Ann to read to her father. So he could get the reading over and done with more quickly, James read one page and then she read one page, and this continued until the book was finished.

Recently, at the beginning of winter, Jean had to go to Brisbane to see a specialist and have surgery, and I went with her. Leaving the house for a week is a mammoth job. I had to do so much planning and organising before I could leave. On my return, I was lying on the bed talking to an old school friend, having some downtime after the busy and stressful time away, when James informed me that the hot water system had broken and they had had no hot water for two days.

'Have you checked the switchboard to see if the system just clicked out?' I said.

He looked at me stupidly. 'Oh, I hadn't thought of that.'

And, sure enough, it had just clicked out.

My friend on the phone was listening to all this and just about wet herself laughing. For two days James and the kids had been enduring cold showers without James once thinking about the simple cause of the problem. I had been home for an hour and the problem was solved. My husband is intelligent, so why, oh why, didn't he think of that?

James and I attempted to go on a trip to Karumba many years ago and we only got as far as fifty kilometres from Normanton before the alternator in the Toyota tray-back broke down, which meant we had no car lights. It made more sense to drive the nearly four hours back home than keep going, as there was more chance of getting the car fixed there. But with no headlights, how were we going to see the road? Well, you guessed it. I had to hang half out the window holding a torch to light our way along the bitumen. It was pure madness, but we made it home in the early hours of the morning.

This incident reminds me of another car incident, when some friends and I were driving around town on our way to another friend's house. The lights in the old Subaru my grandad had given me blew, so we kept driving behind my other friend's car with no lights and only theirs lighting our way.

Years ago, before I went on my overseas trip, I went to visit James in the Northern Territory. During the nine-hour drive, I blew two car tyres. James's cousin Darcy kindly came out with James to help me. It was a great week, with never a dull moment. James decided to introduce me to bush bananas. That was an experience. I had terrible bowel problems for two days, a few close calls, and one code-brown accident. What a great memory to leave my boyfriend with before I set off to go exploring the world for twelve months.

James loves fishing. On the one and only occasion he was able to convince me to go fishing with him in the Northern Territory, I conned Constance, a friend who had been dating Darcy, into coming with us. The four of us drove off into the wilderness to experience fishing and camping.

It wasn't a bad trip over all, and I soon got the hang of baiting my own fishing line. Mind you, we all had a steady amount of alcohol in our system each day to keep us feeling relaxed and mellow. We took along a carton of Watermelon Bacardi Breezers. We could have done with two cartons, as by the end of the trip we had to ration ourselves. I also took my great mate, Southern Comfort, and Constance took a bottle of rum.

After one day's fishing, we were sitting around the campfire after dinner that evening when Darcy and James decided they wanted more rum. We wouldn't give them Constance's stash; we had that very cunningly hidden. We lay in our swags watching the boys search high and low for it.

The next minute James had turned on the chainsaw and they were holding Constance hostage in her swag, threatening her with it, demanding she tell them where her rum was hidden. I raced to the car, turned it on and threatened to drive off, which would have collapsed our entire campsite down around their heads as all the tarps were attached to the car. The boys knew I would do it, so they gave up on the torture-by-chainsaw tactic and jumped in Darcy's yellow Toyota, which was fondly known as 'the sand goanna', and drove around and around in circles, like rally drivers gone mad.

Finally Darcy pulled up and said to Constance, 'Do you wanna come buffalo hunting?'

Really. Such a charming request. Did Darcy really think she'd want to spend even *more* time in his company after the chainsaw incident? I don't think so. Darcy was the last of the true romantics. Eat your heart out, Jane Austin.

We found out later that it was Darcy's standard come-on line. Constance was supposed to be so moved by that offer that she would have jumped lovingly into the front of the car and James would have hopped out. Not surprisingly, she restrained herself and both men got the shits. They drove for two hours to the Borroloola rodeo, leaving us girls alone in the middle of nowhere, and finally returned at daylight.

I think I went stir crazy and the next night I got very drunk. A personality I have not displayed before was unleashed. Jean calls it 'Tara's twenty-sixth'. I proceeded to call James every name under the sun while he lay in his swag, very hungover. I went on and on and on. No one could reason with me. Everyone lay in their swags hoping I would fall asleep with exhaustion at some stage. Darcy did try to use a sweet voice to instil some sense of reason into me, but his words fell on deaf ears. I was giving it to James with full gusto.

That is my one and only fishing trip to date. I'm sure when I go on another one it'll pale by comparison.

James and I went to school together, from year seven till year twelve. I loathed him until year eleven. Something changed in year twelve, when his Scorpio charm took hold. All my school friends have known him for as long as I have, and I think that's why he gets away with half the stuff he does.

For example, one day my friend and I were in the bedroom changing my daughter Ann when she was a baby. James came in twirling a rope in his hand, acting as though he was lassoing out in a paddock. He swung it above his head and next minute it landed around Jean's neck. He pulled Jean back on the bed and Ann flew up in the air. I caught her and went to Jean's rescue. The whole time James was pissing himself laughing.

I attacked him to let Jean go and eventually got the rope off her. She pushed him into a door with all her might and the look on her face, I think it really, really scared him. We were both so furious. Who did he think he was, the lunatic, thinking he could come in and rope grown women, making out it was all a joke, and we wouldn't react this way.

The damage had been done. Jean had rope burns around her neck and had to go to work the next day like that. Of course everyone thought she had gotten lucky and some guy had gone crazy sucking the life out of her neck. You can imagine their disbelief when she protested, saying, 'No, my best friend's husband roped me.'

James doesn't do things like that to me because he knows I don't have a very playful personality and he has to live with me. Jean, however, is more fun and he loves stirring her up and doing stupid things to her, as she bites every time. However, between Jean's mother's Gemini influence and mine, we've been able to teach her not to react. If you don't react to idiots, we tell her, that's half the fun gone for them.

What I've learned about husbands is that if you want a job done, just get on and do it yourself. A husband is like having another child around, just on a larger scale.

9

Soul Mates

Who among us married their soul mate? Or, more truthfully, who will say they *haven't* married their soul mate?

My husband is not my soul mate. I'm not sure if such people even exist, but maybe it's true for some. I love my husband and we will be together forever, God help us, but we don't connect on any deep, mysterious level.

He arrogantly assumes he knows what I'm thinking, but if he really did, he wouldn't do or say half of what comes out of his mouth. One classic example is when we went to a twenty-first birthday party recently. Sometime during the evening, apparently I butted into a conversation he was having and he felt I had disrespected him. I wasn't aware of this and he didn't say anything until we got out to the car, when he let rip. Jean had come to pick us up and we both got a lecture. He went on and on about how I had disrespected him.

I was sitting in the back, thinking I'd had just about as much as I was going to take. The thoughts flitting through my brain were wrong, so wrong. I thought a knife to the throat would end all conversation and he would just shut up.

When we got home I made a cup of tea and had to keep both hands on the cup so I didn't throw hot water all over him. After two minutes he went to bed. It's not normal to feel like doing your husband in so he'll just stop talking or lecturing. It all came down to one question: do I burn him or bleed him? Rum, the root of all evil.

The next morning he was very sore and sorry for himself. He couldn't remember much of what he had said, surprise, surprise, but I promptly reminded him. If he could have read my thoughts he would have realised how close he came to the next life.

He has since vowed he will give up the rum. Yeah, yeah, I've heard that before.

A good friend of mine reassured me by saying, 'It's a Gemini thing, sister. It's quite normal for us Geminis to think quietly about causing them bodily harm if they keep annoying us.'

I do think it must be amazing for those who have married their soul mate to feel that spine-tingling, gut-churning connection of mind, body and spirit. I recently watched a *Twilight* episode and was impressed with the way they had conveyed that connection between the characters. It almost vibrated off the screen. I've seen many movies in my life, and in *Twilight* they definitely had a connection.

I'm a pragmatic person, however, and I know, alas, that life isn't as it's portrayed in the movies. I'm grateful to have a husband who loves me, and who works hard to provide for his family. If I have to share something, he's usually the first person I want to phone and discuss it with, even if it does annoy him sometimes, as he's always so busy at work.

Many years ago Jean, Constance and I went to Boulia Camel Races, travelling with an Irish nurse. We were chatting away as usual, which is never hard for me once I'm on a roll, and the nurse asked me if James was my soul mate.

I looked at Constance. 'I'll leave you to answer that,' I said.

Even back then, Constance could answer that he wasn't. Not that that's a bad thing. If most people are honest they would probably acknowledge they haven't married their soul mate, which doesn't mean they're not living a fulfilled and happy life together of course.

What I've learned about relationships, whether or not you believe someone is a soul mate, is that if someone comes along and ticks all the boxes that are most important to you, you should go for it. Life is too short to wait around for that mysterious 'something' we read about in books or see in the movies, which has, after all, evolved from someone else's imagination. That's the beauty of books and movies—they stimulate our imaginations and provide escapism from reality for an hour or two.

10

Sex

Men and women are so different when it comes to sex. Men are such visual creatures, and they can 'do it' without much thought at all, whereas we females are thinkers and require a bit more effort.

Well, some of us, that is.

I have a friend who lived like a man before she had children. Her boyfriend couldn't keep up with her. I always knew if she'd had had sex before working a night shift. If she was happy, we'd have a good shift, but if her boyfriend had been 'too tired' to perform before she came to work she was a nightmare to be around.

But getting back to me. I walked into the house recently after working in my gift shop. James had come home early from work. There was stuff everywhere in the dining room, dishes piled up in the sink, and do you think he was helping to clean up? Oh no. He was in the bedroom, singing out to me.

When I went down there, he was waiting for 'it'. 'Are you ready?' he asked me.

Ready? You have to be kidding me. He was lying back on the bed, waiting for me to cope with the household chaos unaided and then feel like sex. Was he crazy?

I just walked out. I had so many jobs to do I couldn't think straight, and he thought I could just drop everything for sex. Oh no. It doesn't work that way. All I wanted to do after I finally got things sorted out was relax on the couch in front of my favourite show and dream of McDreamy. Yes, I love *Grey's Anatomy* and think Derek Shepherd is so yummy. I would let him work on more than my brain anytime.

Had I walked in to find James doing the washing up and the kitchen bench clean, then we might have got somewhere, as that would have been like foreplay to me. I'm a simple woman with simple needs. Just keep it basic. Cook dinner, wash up, bath the kids, put them to bed and I will go down to the bedroom and wait for you. That's all that would need to happen and he'd be on a sure thing.

Why doesn't my husband get that?

I've always wondered why James is always so horny the day after a big night out, and I also wonder if all men are like that. He always wants to have sex when he's hungover, and I often have the feeling that he wouldn't really care with whom or even with what. He just needs to have his basic needs taken care of. I, on the other hand, refuse to be used like a vessel and flat out say 'No, no and no'.

Don't get me wrong. Many times I've given him sex to keep the peace, or have taken one for the team so we girls can have a night out. Then he'll stay at home, relaxed and content. But there's something about the day after a night out that lights his fire, especially if he arrived home full of cheek and bad manners, which thankfully hasn't happened for a while. The usual routine is for him to come home stewing over something I've said, wanting to psychoanalyse it for hours and hours, to the point where I feel like physically putting him out of his misery.

I've spoken to a few girlfriends about this and they've all said the same thing: some hang-over horniness comes over a man after a night out, and all they want to do, once they've finished feeling sorry for themselves at the shit that perpetually pours out of their mouths, is to have sex. Meanwhile we've been up for hours attending to *our* children while he slept on, and the last thing on our minds is giving them pleasure.

Do men really think that really works for us? You have a hand. Feel free to use it.

I've always been a firm believer in the two F's: feed them and F*@# them. Do these two things and you can't go wrong. That covers their two basic needs of existence.

I hear feminists screaming loudly at these words; however, I don't personally see the point of James having to miss out just because I'm not in the mood, or because I'm not going to get an orgasm from it. I've spoken about this to different women through the years and some think like me while others only have sex if they're going to orgasm as well. It's a personal choice, but I think my husband is pleased I'm not the latter because he knows that if he waited for me to feel like it all the time he would be waiting a long time.

James and I are total opposites on the odd occasions when we can go away without the children. He'll be doing high-fives and nearly sprinting out the door. Kids? What kids? But by day two he can't wait to get home to them. 'Wonder what the kids are doing,' he'll say repeatedly.

I know I'm going to miss them, and so I become emotional and sad when we leave. But by day two I'm booked in for a spa treatment and having my two cocktails, thinking I might even try each one on the cocktail menu. I'll be thinking, I don't have to get up to kids in the morning. Yippy woo-hoo, this is the life. I must've been mad to think I would miss them.

So, yeah, I get a taste of freedom and think yep, yep, this is not too bad. I can actually go to the toilet without someone coming in to ask me a question. Thomas even tries to climb up on my lap and is so helpful that he gets the toilet paper and wants to help me wipe my bum.

When we're away I really get into sex and lose myself in the moment, as opposed to constantly thinking that any minute the kids are going to unlock the door with a knife and come in. Or they'll wake up, come in, and because it's dark climb into our bed and be none the wiser.

I'm not sure about other women, but for me, having that concern on my mind takes away from the moment. James, on the other hand, couldn't give a shit, and could get his rocks off in a cyclone with the threat of the roof about to be ripped off.

In the past I've said to him, 'Seriously, as long as there's a hole, and it feels nice and cosy, it wouldn't worry you.' He feigns horror at this, but it's true, especially after he's had a night out.

What I've learned about men and sex is to keep it basic and simple. Rub that brain between their legs and they're ready at the drop of a hat. Most of us women, however, need our minds to be in the mood. I've learned through the years that sometimes when I don't entirely feel like it, and it's been a few days, I should initiate it when it suits me instead of waiting for my husband to pester me for sex just as I'm about to sit down and watch my favourite TV show. On those occasions I've found that seven times out of ten I enjoy it as much as him. Also, it's over and done with before the TV show starts.

My motto: the two F's.

11

Masturbation

*M*asturbation is a touchy topic, especially among women; it's not something we openly discuss. But I was fortunate in that I grew up with a group of girls who discussed sex as naturally as we talked about the weather. We were all at an age where we were losing our virginity, and whispered conversations during class in the library became a lot more interesting than learning economics. My apologies to my economics teacher but it's true. But still, masturbation wasn't something we discussed at any length.

After leaving school I made some of my closest and dearest friends when I went nursing. We would discuss men, but to suggest that we masturbated was out of the question, until of course we'd had one too many drinks. Then the conversation became colourful regarding who owned a vibrator or dildo. I used to be horrified at the mere suggestion that I had one. Who,

11 MASTURBATION

me? My prim-and-proper personality came into play. God forbid I would ever have such a thing.

In all honesty, I didn't have one in those days. Jean and Fay bought one for me as a joke. Some joke. I would have needed internal surgery at the mere thought of it. It was way, way too big for this girl. Another year Jean and Fay gave me a pack of small colourful ones. My middle finger could have given me more pleasure than those things. One of my good friends, a male colleague at work, spread them all out on the nurses' desk on Christmas day.

My overseas trip broadened my mind in many ways. While in Canada, a friend told me about 'rabbit ears'. I was intrigued.

'The first time you masturbate,' she said, 'you have to stick with it until you relax and reach your full potential. Otherwise how will you know what you want from a man if you don't even know yourself what brings you pleasure?'

So I went home with eyes like fried eggs after my education on bringing pleasure to myself.

Many years went by until the fateful day that Jean and Fay gave me 'blue boy'. I was now the owner of my very own rabbit ears. Anyone who knows me is aware that I'm always busy, so how the hell was I going to find some spare time in my day to introduce myself to blue boy? I felt this sense of guilt, wondering if I could be accused of cheating on my husband if I used it.

So I killed two birds with one stone. I already have to take time out for sex with my husband, so why not introduce blue boy? Needless to say, the rest is history.

My point is that something has made a once-shy, reserved girl in her twenties bloom into the woman I am today. I don't advertise the fact that I have a vibrator, but I no longer feel embarrassed at the suggestion of it, and nor do I deny it if asked. There's nothing to be embarrassed about. It's okay to own your sexuality and be comfortable with it.

A friend told me once, or tried to tell me, that her husband didn't masturbate. OMG, was she really that naive? She was a relatively smart woman, so her innocent outlook amazed me. She said he didn't need to because he had her. Yeah, right. With the amount of times they think of sex, most men are like our rooster that madly terrorises our hens all day. My husband is in awe of his efforts.

When this friend told me she can sometimes go weeks without having sex with her husband, I said, 'Of *course* he masturbates if he goes without sex for weeks. Of *course* he's going to touch the one thing that gives him pleasure.' Either she was in denial or stupid.

She said she was going to ask him. Well, I knew how that would go. He obviously didn't feel comfortable in telling her that he masturbated, even though they had been married for over ten years. If they didn't already have that type of honest communication about sex, I didn't think it was going to start now. This was a woman who had had her fair share of lovers, and she honestly didn't think her husband would do that.

The same friend told me she didn't own a vibrator, and that her husband would be horrified if she pulled one out and would most likely feel threatened by it.

'Well,' I told her, 'that's easily solved. If it's that important just get one that's smaller than his own appendage so he doesn't feel inferior.'

It's not like masturbation is a secret. There wouldn't be a male alive that hasn't masturbated at some stage in their lives. I'm always surprised when women deny, often emphatically, that their boyfriend or husband masturbates. I look at them like they have horns sprouting from their heads, as that must be what's affecting their brain.

What I've learned about masturbation through the years is that it's okay. It's okay to be sexual. We should own our sexuality, and be clear and concise on what gives us pleasure and be able to communicate this. We have to be able to communicate with our lovers.

12

Pregnancy and Babies

Being pregnant for the first time is a wonderful experience, and being able to share it with family and friends is really special. The first time, when everything is new, we usually do it by the book, from attending antenatal classes and reading baby books on everything about what's happening with your body each week of every trimester, to names and their meanings.

I remember being at work one night and choosing names with a couple of friends. They would each put a mark next to their favourites. One of them was a lot older than me and was so funny in the way she broke down my list according to rhyme. For example, I like Adelaide as a name, but she looked at me and said, 'Gatorade.' Charlotte rhymed with Harlot, and so on.

I thought I'd never choose a name, but eventually we chose Henry. It really doesn't matter what name you choose; someone always has a comment. I had unwittingly named Henry after my great-grandfather on my father's side, whom I had thought was Robert. This also meant that my dad's cousin, known to me as Uncle Bobby, was actually named Henry.

When I was pregnant I was so sick that some days I didn't think I could move. The 24/7 nausea and extreme exhaustion were all consuming.

Sometimes at work, when I couldn't function a minute longer, I would get into my scrubs and hide in the theatre. I knew that by the time someone got dressed and came in I would have time to get off the floor. One day I wasn't quick enough and the theatre nurse caught me. Thankfully she was a friend, and even though I was busted I wasn't in trouble. I think she worked out what was wrong, but she was very good and kept my secret for a few more weeks until the infamous twelve-week mark, after which the nausea ceased.

I had arranged a fortieth birthday celebration for a friend a week before. Everyone assumed I was guzzling cocktails and no one even noticed I was going up and ordering my own drinks. They were all 'mocktails'. I didn't do too badly, as by five am I was still standing, while three other non-pregnant friends had piked out and gone to bed hours before. There was me, newly pregnant, with a woman in her fifties, another lady in her thirties, and the birthday boy.

You can imagine their surprise a week later when I said I was pregnant. I couldn't have hidden it much longer. I was hard-pressed to fit into my jeans. Little did I know at the time that I was growing a baby sumo.

Through the months I continued to grow beyond anyone's expectations for a first-time mum.

I did the usual first-time pregnancy thing and sent off photos to family and friends. One aunt emailed back, asking, 'How many are in there?'

The first time Henry kicked felt like a little miracle. James was off with his mates playing five hundred. I phoned to let him know, and within ten minutes I heard the door open and he was home, full of excitement and ready to feel our baby kick. True to form, the baby did not kick for his father that night.

By the fourth pregnancy I don't think James even attempted to feel it kick. Poor number three and four babies.

Jean came with me to antenatal classes, as did James, my man's man of a husband. A friend of mine took the classes, and James tortured her by asking numerous embarrassing questions. Thank goodness we knew everyone else there.

Much to James's annoyance, I didn't get really horny during the middle trimester, which is what we had been told might happen. We waited and waited, but alas, my libido did not miraculously skyrocket. By the fourth baby we gave up all hope of me turning into any nymphomaniac sex kitten with a well-rounded bump out the front.

I'm sure I'm not the only woman to have done this, but I pickled my little darlings. One of my good friends was housesitting when I was pregnant with Henry, our first child, and there was a pool. There we were, having a jolly time guzzling colourful drinks and, bonus for us, the bottle shop was right next door so we could skip over there wringing wet for more booze.

I do vaguely remember James asking, 'What if you're pregnant?' and I chortled back, 'Oh well, it's pickled then, isn't it?'

Two weeks later I knew I was pregnant. We had been trying for a while, but after seven months we thought we were being too regimented and just needed to get back to having fun and all would fall into place. So in my defence I think all the laughing, chilling with friends, and copious amounts of colourful drinks over the festive season helped all the ingredients fall into place. I think I can nail actual moment of conception for all four children, as they were pretty special times, as opposed to a ho-hum, do-my-duty type of moment.

Two weeks before my due date I travelled down to Townsville by train. I was like a travelling whale. I stayed with one of my best mates for one week and James turned up the next week.

Seeing my obstetrician was like visiting the school principal after being caught doing something naughty, but the minute I became an inpatient she was amazing. She looked like she would take no prisoners, but that was no longer directed at me but at the nurses, who scurried around like mice about to be pounced upon.

She gave me the best advice. 'Everyone is going to be full of opinions on how you and your husband should take care of your baby,' she said, 'but just smile and thank them.' She said that sometimes the advice would be helpful, but most of the time we should just take bits and pieces here and there, and do what worked for us. 'It's a learning process, as babies all have their own individual personalities. It's a time for you all to get to know each other.'

She was so right. Henry was a laidback baby who tolerated the controlled-crying method. It only took us two nights when he was eleven months of age and, you little beauty, he was sleeping through the night.

When I had Ann, our second child, the obstetrician reminded me not to have rigid routine, as what worked for one baby might not necessarily work for the next one. Truer words were never spoken. Even as babies all four children were individuals. What worked with one did not work with another, and we had to be flexible and adjust ourselves accordingly.

When James turned up in Townsville he laughed to see me so huge. Of course, once I had Henry it all made sense.

We checked into the Queensland Country Women's Association units at Kissing Point, and Megan flew in from Sale in Victoria the next day with my gorgeous niece, Joyce. We just chilled for the week, with walks along The Strand.

I am unable to let people down. Once I've said I'm going to do something I have to follow through. The Oktoberfest was on the weekend we were there, so two days before my due date my good friend Cate and I went to the Oktoberfest. She had never been to one before so I didn't want to let her down.

I had gone shopping in the morning and by the time I got home from the shops I had conjunctivitis. I asked James to take me swimming in the seawater, hoping the salt would help. It didn't, so we had to go to one of those seven-day clinics. By that time I had copious amounts of goo gushing from my eye. Imagine how I looked going to the Oktoberfest. I picked up Cate and we had a lot of fun, goopy eyes and all. I danced and had random people feeling my belly and for a brief moment I felt like me.

On the Sunday James and Megan were pressuring me to deliver this baby, although Henry wasn't due until the Monday. As always, James needed to get back to work, so on Monday we went to a naturopath, who massaged in certain spots, and gave me some vile concoction to drink and rub on my tummy.

By that stage, if I sat down it was a hell of a job to get me up. At four am on Tuesday morning I thought I needed to do a wee, which turned out to be quite a large one. After a couple of hours I got James to take me to the hospital and he reacted like Mr Bean. He drove into some roadworks and had to turn around, and then he went to the wrong hospital. We finally arrived at the Mater after dropping off my niece at my friend's home. The doctor arrived about eight am and examined me. I was only two centimetres dilated, four hours after my waters had broken.

I should have realised then that I wasn't progressing too well. Much to my annoyance, I hadn't been able to use the spa. I got as far as trying to use the bouncy ball when James wondered aloud how many other women in labour had bounced on it, and whether it was cleaned well between times. So I was resigned to pacing corridors and taking hot showers.

I could hear James and Megan tossing up as to whose turn it was to rub my back, as if it was a major inconvenience to them. This continued until eight pm, when I was given an epidural. I'm petrified of needles, so to curl up in a ball in pain while someone shoved a needle in my spine was not my idea of fun.

My sister hid behind the curtain and couldn't watch. The anaesthetist saw her and told her not to be such a scaredy cat. James thought he was talking to me and nearly bit his head off.

When I was relaxed, and finally fully dilated, I pushed my heart out for nearly two hours with no success. Henry just wasn't budging, so I was wheeled off to have a caesarean birth. Megan was keeping the family in Brisbane up to date and Aunty Bella was worried sick.

It was no fun being in there. My legs started shaking and I couldn't stop them. The contractions didn't stop long enough for them to get to Henry. They were thinking of alternatives when, in one swift moment, my obstetrician was able to get him.

James was becoming anxious. They asked him to leave the room as they were about to put me under general anaesthetic. At last we heard a baby cry. James told me later that if he had had to choose which of us to save in an emergency, it would have been me, as he thought we could always have another baby. He was a total mess.

Thankfully we became proud parents. On the Tuesday, at ten pm, I gave birth to a beautiful, healthy blue-eyed blond baby boy. Henry weighed 10 pounds 5 ounces. He was 58 centimetres long and the circumference of his head was 38 centimetres. Two years earlier, my father had died on a Tuesday at ten pm, an unhealthy blue-eyed blond, and in different months. Both were born in the year of the horse.

The nurses came in that night to say that Henry wouldn't settle with water and asked if they could give him some formula. I told them to go ahead as I was too exhausted to care. When it came to breastfeeding, I was so fortunate to have a hungry boy who latched on and never looked back. I'm a pretty casual person over some things, and I didn't get caught up in the whole nipple confusion. If a baby is hungry it will latch on and feed and they don't care where it will come from, which was the case in my situation. Once Henry became hungry, he had no problems with nipple confusion. Mind you, after having free rein at his own dairy bar there were a couple of times when I had expressed and he would not have a bar of it.

I even had a child-health nurse tell me to give him some formula, as he was such a big baby. She was old school and a family friend so I tried, and you know what? It didn't stay down long. He projectile vomited the whole lot.

I didn't feel that overwhelming mother love when I was in hospital as I'd expected, but I knew that was normal. Some women are talkers like me and chat about everything, and a friend had told me how she had felt exactly the same after going through a long labour, followed by an emergency caesarean birth. It took her about two weeks before the mother–baby bond really kicked in, but she said that when it did she would have killed for that baby.

I knew it would kick in for me as well, but my obstetrician was worried, as she knew I hadn't wanted a caesarean birth. I was very upset by it and James kept shoving the baby in my face.

Coming home in the car ten days later, that overwhelming unconditional love hit me in a wave and I knew I would love this tiny human being until the day I died. But on the down side, I learned that taking an eight-hour drive in a car after major abdominal surgery isn't the best move. I was bent like a boomerang by the time we got home. Consequently, with the next three babies I always flew home.

I had Ann, our second child, ten days day before my due date. When I found out I was pregnant with her I realised that once again I had unknowingly attempted to pickle her. I had just finished my nursing degree, and hadn't seen James for quite a few weeks. My cousin got married a couple of months later, and I flew down to Brisbane for the wedding. There I was catching up with family, with my study finished and a toddler at home with Dad. To save money, I bunked with my male cousin and my female cousin's husband and boyfriend, so I was basically baching it.

The day of the wedding I had to direct my cousin's husband to the other side of Brisbane to collect his suit. What a drama. He was Irish and hadn't been in Brisbane long, and coming from a country town I was out of my depth as well. We managed to keep our cool, survived the drive, retrieved the suit and, surprisingly, arrived in time.

The wedding was beautiful, but try as I might I just couldn't get drunk, no matter how much red wine I drank. It was like my body was repelling it. I so wanted to kick my heels up and party.

I went out after the wedding but not for long. I should have suspected something was wrong, as I was also very tired. In fact, I felt totally exhausted, but I put it down to a busy schedule. After the wedding, I went with a close friend to O'Reilly's National Park and tried once again to guzzle cocktails, but in the end gave up.

After a very hectic few days, I was back home again. I was cleaning out the shed with Constance's help when Jean turned up, took one look at me and said, 'You're pregnant.'

I laughed it off, but it was Jean who had predicted I would be pregnant with Henry by a certain time and that I would have blue-eyed blond son, so deep down I was thinking she could be right. Sure enough, the next time I was at work I did a pregnancy test and it was positive.

Well, I just cried and cried, as I was not ready to be pregnant again; I had been so busy doing my degree that I just wanted to spend more time with Henry.

I phoned Jean and Fay, and they were so happy. They kept saying it was meant to be. I was howling down the phone. The tears lasted a few weeks on and off, until I adjusted to my new condition. I also kept wondering how I'd love another child as much as I loved the one I had.

Those thoughts brought back a memory of a conversation I had had with my dad. When one of my best friends was pregnant with her second child, she had expressed the same concerns and my dad had assured her that when the baby arrived love would come with it.

So I held onto those words while the pregnancy hormones turned me into the anti-Christ. No longer was I the sweet-natured person I had been when pregnant with Henry. James and I did not have one fight throughout that first pregnancy, but with this little fire-sign baby growing inside of me I was in a perpetual state of pre-menstrual syndrome. One of my friends said that I had to be having a girl, as I was so bloody irritable.

I remember reading about urinary-tract infections bringing on early labour. At twenty-two weeks I had a urinary-tract infection. The doctor gave me antibiotics to nip the contractions in the bud, as I was a planned caesarean delivery after the drama with Henry and was not supposed to be experiencing contractions.

Ann was born twelve days early and thank goodness, as she weighed 9 pounds 13 ounces. It was a textbook caesarean birth and she looked absolutely beautiful. I couldn't believe it when I woke up in recovery and they said I had a big beautiful girl.

I had had a general anaesthetic by choice, as the thought of having a needle put in my back again was not an option for me. This time I hadn't been in pain with full-on contractions, as I had been when having Henry and I would have been lying there cold turkey. I don't regret my decision to have a general anaesthetic with the three subsequent babies.

The health professionals tried to tell me I might have attachment issues if I had a general anaesthetic, but it's a personal choice and I knew if they tried forcing me to have an epidural, there really would be issues.

James had to wait just outside the theatre door. First the staff took the baby to be checked by the paediatrician, and then James went to the nursery with the midwife.

When I woke up I was taken back to my room and given my baby. After the non-complicated delivery, I was in love from the minute I first saw her. My dad may not have been alive, but his words still resonated with me. As he had said, the love just flows no matter how many kids you have.

I flew home with Ann. No eight-hour drive home for me this time. When Jean picked me up at the airport, she said I must have the wrong baby. Ann had a touch of jaundice; she was a huge butterball, with yellow skin and a head of black hair. The nurses had said she looked like a china doll.

Ann's birth was my only non-complicated delivery, as the last two boys insisted on making their pregnancies and deliveries memorable.

William, our third child, was a holiday baby. I fell pregnant with him on a holiday in England and Canada and, once again, without knowing it, I pickled him. I wasn't expecting to be pregnant, and when we stayed with a friend from my earlier travelling days we went out on the razzle-dazzle until four am. Imagine my surprise when I found out I was expecting again.

I woke up late the next morning feeling like crap, which never happens to me. I don't suffer from hangovers, as a rule, so I should have suspected something while we were travelling, as I had been experiencing extreme tiredness. I kept putting it down to jet lag, plus we had three little kids with us as we had taken my gorgeous niece Joyce travelling as well. Being older than Henry, she was like our first girl, and we had been such a large part of her life for the first six years. So on our trip we had Joyce, aged six, Henry, aged four, and Ann, who was nearly two.

In hindsight, dragging everyone overseas wasn't our smartest move. It set us back financially, but my emotions had the better of me. I just needed to see all my overseas friends again and so badly wanted to spend Christmas with Anne, my friend in Canada.

A week after we landed in Canada the nausea set in and I started vomiting. That was all I needed. My over-stretched stomach muscles couldn't hold the baby in, and my belly popped out. So we had the added expense of having to buy some maternity clothes.

Apparently I resemble Madonna. Many, many people have passed comment on the resemblance. I don't see it myself, but others do. We were in Canada, with me feeling like death, and looking drained of energy, when the woman at the ice cream stand nearly had a fit when I walked up to order ice creams.

Really, I looked like crap. I had three kids dragging behind me and James is no Guy Richie. How she could possibly think that I was Madonna was beyond me. Did she think I was using the kids and James as a disguise? The guy standing next to me checked me out to see what all the fuss was about.

I remember coming home from Canada and not wanting to tell anyone I was pregnant, not that I could hide it. Although I always knew I wanted four children, everyone else thought I should stop at two. Consequently I wasn't given an overly joyous reception when people realised the bump under my clothes wasn't fat put on from the Christmas holidays.

However, William turned out to be the baby everyone wanted. He was so calm and angelic. Women would tell me that if they were guaranteed a baby like William they would fall pregnant tomorrow. He was a placid baby. I could feed him and put him in his cot, and he would just go to sleep.

Ann, on the other hand, let her intentions be known from an early age. No amount of controlled-crying was going to work with her. She was the boss and that was it. So we learned from an early age with Ann to pick the battles we could win. If we couldn't win we didn't even bother trying, as we couldn't give her a win. That took me back to my first obstetrician's advice: do what you have to do to survive. I must have done okay, as I had two more babies after Ann, and she is now nine and still living.

William was such a big baby that I was measuring forty weeks pregnant when in fact I was only thirty-seven weeks. I had to make a quick trip to the nearby town for an ultrasound to make sure all was okay, and both my GP and obstetrician wanted me in Townsville. I was in the middle of organising a sixtieth luncheon for my mother, and a nurse colleague was coming out for a surprise visit to attend the gathering, so there was no way I was going anywhere until that was over. Nothing annoys me more than plans disrupted. I finally put my doctor out of his misery and got myself to Townsville.

William arrived by caesarean section, eighteen days before my due date. Poor old William didn't look like a textbook caesarean baby. He had cuts behind his ear and his face looked a bit worse for wear. Apparently they had had to use forceps on him.

William was my sanity. He was number three and what an absolute delight he was. I thought Henry was relaxed but, honestly, if you could bottle what William floats around on you would be rich. He is so easy-going and sensitive and loving. He can also be very quiet, and if we let him he would fly under the radar. I used to have people say to me that if they could be guaranteed a baby like William they would have one tomorrow.

One night when a friend was over and I finished feeding him, put him into his cot and closed the door.

She just looked at me. 'Is that it?' she said. 'You don't have to pat him?'

'I know how cruisy this is,' I said, ' because I had to pat the first two.'

I think it was because by the time William came along he just had to wait. I would be getting the first two out of the bath and organised, and William would be crying, but I just had to sort the toddlers out first. Then I could sit down and see to his needs, and sometimes he just went to sleep. Even to this day, one minute William can be talking to you and the next he's asleep, and in a deep sleep. You wonder how on earth that kid can fall asleep so quickly. A bomb could go off around him and it wouldn't bother him.

Thomas, our last child, had me sick for nearly twenty weeks. I coughed so badly I nearly needed to invest in old people's incontinence pads. My mother suggested I wear them to my grandmother's funeral, which I declined, although I did take extra pants. We were building our family house throughout Thomas's pregnancy, which meant for a busy time.

Pregnancy taught me that having babies is such an amazing journey, but it's never entirely easy. I'm sure that those women who have babies that sleep through the night and say everything is so damn wonderful are covering up for how bloody exhausted they really are. The first twelve weeks are the worst, while mother and baby are working each other out and developing a routine that works for them both. Every baby is different.

It's okay to say you're exhausted and sometimes the baby's crying drives you nuts. On one occasion when Henry crying incessantly, it was driving me so nuts that I went outside, closed the door, and hung the clothes on the line for five or ten minutes just to have time out from the crying. He was safe, he couldn't get out, and no harm was coming to him. I just needed to walk away, regroup and then come back and see to him.

What I've learned about babies is that only a small percentage of them sleep through the night when they first go home. So when some mums paint this rosy picture and behave like Stepford wives, I smile and think, yeah, right, just be honest and stop trying to make the rest of us feel inadequate, because we're not. It's perfectly normal to run the daily gamut of emotions, and be exhausted and frustrated with the chaos around us. It doesn't last forever; there is light at the end of the tunnel.

13

Our Children

There's something magical and unconditional about the love we feel for our children. Well, I do at least. It's a love like no other. You know without a doubt that you would do anything for them. It's completely engulfing.

But OMG, my kids are so uncivilised. One day I dropped them at tennis class before school and when I went to the school to give them their lunches, Ann informed me that Henry had hit her across the face with his tennis racket. I went to Henry's class to give him his lunch and quietly whispered in his ear, asking why he had hit his sister in the face. He informed me that she had hit him first.

I discovered all of this after doing reading group with William. I looked around and noticed that Thomas was doing the Niagara Falls of pees on the cemented lunch area.

Off I marched to the prep room, grabbed a bucket and washed the pee away as best I could. The principal came out so I explained the puddle of water. This was day two of Thomas 'marking his territory', so to speak, as the day before he had peed in the prep playground.

The principal's reply was, 'The world is a man's urinal.'

Don't I know it.

My boys have always been quite uninhibited when nature calls; they pull up anywhere outside and just pee. They really only need something to discreetly hide behind and away they go.

The two big boys go outside every morning and pee over the veranda. We have three toilets in our house, so why do they do this? Does the veranda seem more appealing? Henry used to do it over the front veranda rail until his father complained about the urine smell every time he came up the front steps, so now Henry goes out to the back veranda. He kept peeing on one of his father's plants and it started to wilt.

Boys are so fixated on their penis from an early age. Why is that? Henry, at the age of three, used to see how far he could pee and if he could pee on his baby sister's head. Thomas tries to use his penis as a gun and chases the other kids, pretending to shoot them.

Henry is a dramatist at times and a worrywart. Once when we were on holiday at the beach he was bitten by something. I initially thought he might have been scratched by a shell, but he came screaming up to me saying his arm was burning and announced he was going to die. Initially I couldn't stop laughing, but when the inside of his arm started developing welts I got concerned—for about a minute. He was making too much noise for someone about to die from anything poisonous.

All the way home he kept asking me how it feels when you die (like I'd know). 'Do I go to the light, Mum?' he said.

Had he been listening to too many friends, or watching too many movies? He willed his Skylanders to William, and convinced him that he was dying. I had to explain to William that Henry was making far too much noise for someone who was dying. After a shower, an application of pawpaw ointment and an antihistamine tablet, Henry lay down in front of the TV and miraculously lived for another day.

Last year Henry slid behind with his schooling halfway through the first semester, so we gave him the job of cleaning pipes underneath the house with a hose — with very, very smelly goo coming out of them as the pipes under the sink were blocked. His father stood there giving him instructions, explaining to him in true James style that if his schoolwork didn't improve he was only going to be qualified to clean pipes when he grew up. After that Henry's schoolwork improved dramatically.

On another occasion Henry had to trim trees along our dirt road in the middle of summer. He was armed with sunscreen, hat and water bottle, and that job didn't impress him either. When I drove down the road I saw the sorry sight of a bunch of kids looking like a prison gang doing hard labour. The other kids had felt sorry for him, especially Ann, and had gone to help him out.

This may not be the way to impose discipline according to the touted how-to parenting books, but it worked for Henry. He went on to show greatly improved results in his schoolwork and had an amazing second semester that year. He received an A for the first time on a maths test, and received numerous neat-bookwork nominations and an award.

The pre-teen years are upon Henry now, and last year he started to backchat me a lot, which was hard for me as he has always been a good boy. As he was my first child, I'm sure I've spoilt him—James is always saying I have—but if lavishing him with love, hugs and kisses is spoiling then I would spoil him again in a heartbeat. Heaven only knows what's in store for me when the teenage years truly kick in, but so far, even when we're experiencing tough days, what Henry and I do have is communication, which I have encouraged from his first day at kindy.

Ann will sometimes terrorise her brothers, claiming that I favour the boys over her. She will sometimes start by saying that I hate her, love the boys more, pick on her, and I'm mean to her. Yeah, that's right.

'Mum, I'm dumb,' she said to me once. 'I know that's what you think. I must be adopted. This is what adopted people feel like. I might as well get a knife stab myself, you'll all be happy then.'

This outburst came about because she couldn't spell her words and I told her to study them again. She then started shoving and hitting Thomas because he looked at her the wrong way. I wondered, is this normal behaviour for a nine-year-old girl? I couldn't tolerate her behaviour. I actually sent James a text: *You have to sort Ann out. She is terrorising us.*

As if James has nothing better to do than get texts from his deranged wife. He only has a department to run and a budget worth millions to manage. I forgot about that because right then, at that precise moment in time, my needs were greater. Nothing was more important than the fact that his daughter was driving us all nuts. At seven-thirty in the morning. I stood there trying to use my sweet voice with her, thinking the whole time that a mouth gag wouldn't go astray.

At moments like this I think: this is what my life is reduced to, this cheeky child back-chatting me, full of dramatics. I don't feel old enough to be her mum. Can't I return her and catch the next plane and go travelling—preferably somewhere that has a day spa.

All the mums out there with young children should enjoy it while it lasts, as the older children get, the more attitude they develop. It just pours out when they're frustrated, not as a nice slow drip but as a full-on burst water main.

I just love the advice that some mums have given me. For instance, 'Have you tried time out?' My reply (in my head) is: *Have you tried standing in front of a runaway train thinking you'll survive?*

I try, calmly, to get Ann to be reasonable and if that fails I ask her to stay in her room until she can speak nicely. I'm a big believer in actions having consequences, so I let her know that if she continues down the path she's chosen she'll miss out on doing things.

Obviously, Ann has a fiery personality. It might have something to do with her being a Sagittarius, with her moon sign in Leo, and that her Chinese sign is Monkey.

Thankfully, though, she's not a sulker. After an explosion she's usually over it in minutes. She can rage at me and love me, all in a ten-minute timeframe. She's a funny kid; she thinks it's okay if *she* argues with me, but heaven help anyone else if they're cheeky to her mother. She'll immediately leap to my defence.

Overall, Ann is amazingly organised for her age and can be a very good help at home in getting things done.

Ann was hard to tolerate from the age of two to four, but I knew this was okay after talking to a friend whose children were older than mine. She is a very open and honest mother who has never painted it as a bed of roses.

'There are just some stages through your kids' lives,' she said, 'when you get on with one or two personalities more than the others, and that's okay as it'll eventually get better. It's not that you love one more than the other, it's just that you might clash with a particular kid's personality at that particular time.'

When Ann turned four something clicked and I started to enjoy my daughter again. I learned to appreciate her good points and to try work with the negative by looking for a positive.

We now get on most of the time. She still fires off the handle, and attacks first and thinks later, but at least it's only at home. When she first started prep, her fiery little disposition had her getting into a bit of trouble, but after introducing the chill-out tent, where she had somewhere to go before exploding, it made a big difference.

That chill-out tent got a lot of use in the beginning, but by halfway through prep she didn't need it anymore. I was so proud of her for being able to develop self-control, even if it was only at school.

William, our third child, has always been my sanity. He has such a beautiful temperament and so far is no problem, although I remember Henry being a lovely, gentle, quiet boy, too, until halfway through year one, when he started to develop a bit of attitude.

As a baby, I could feed William, put him into the cot and he would put himself to sleep. I didn't even have to pat his back. I think it had something to do with me being busy getting the older ones out of the bath, or trying to get them organised so I could sit down with William. By the time I got William he would have self-soothed.

William has red hair, and for some strange reason, ever since he could talk he would be most upset if anyone called him a redhead. 'It's brown,' he would say.

Halfway through year one, a girl joined his class and her hair was red. He came home that day and told me there was a girl in his class with orange hair like him. So for some time his hair was orange and now we've moved onto red — on his terms. I've explained to him how special it is to have red hair as not many people have red hair anymore.

William is quiet and takes things in that you don't even realise he's noticed. He surprises me with his observations and his questions. For example, he asked me one day, 'Do black people have black ears?" Where that question came from I don't know; it was purely innocent, and something that obviously intrigued him. That's William; he comes out with the most random questions.

Children are innocent when it comes to colour. I remember Henry coming home from kindy and telling me he had a 'black' friend. I was taken aback and wondered what he meant. When I got to the bottom of it, I found out he meant hair colour. Yes, this boy, who is still a great mate today, is aboriginal and does have brown skin. But Henry hadn't noticed his skin colour; he just knew that he had 'white' (blond) hair and his friend had 'black' hair.

Luckily I knew the mum, and I explained to her that if she heard Henry saying that her son was 'black', it was simply because of his hair colour.

She laughed. 'Not to worry,' she said, 'it's just the innocence of kids.'

Like William, Thomas, our youngest, has a wicked sense of humour, and when he smiles his eyes light up with mischief. He is a Taurus and can be very stubborn and very bossy, which can take a bit of reigning in at times, but we just have to work with our kids' personalities.

I'm big believer in star signs. Thomas is a Taurus, so tackling him head on is not going to work; if he has a temper tantrum we have to distract him. It has taken four kids to get one who's helpful to me. Thomas is the only one who will come out and help me bring in the grocery bags from the car, and he's the only one who will shut the cupboard doors behind him.

I believe in letting kids explore their personalities without restriction, so the day Thomas wanted to wear his pyjamas to kindy I let him. He was only three and not causing any harm to anyone. We had to do reading group in William's class first. When we walked in, the other mothers and kids checked him out in his robot flannel PJs, which gave William's teacher the idea of throwing a pyjama party for the last day of school.

Another time Thomas walked into school wearing an eye mask up on his forehead; he wore that for days. Then I bought him short dinosaur pyjamas, which he also wore to school. It was quite a battle to get them off him every afternoon so I could wash them. He's at prep school this year and has to conform to a uniform, which is why I've been happy for him to wear what he wants to kindy. I know that when he goes to prep, he won't be able to.

What I've learned from my children is that they are all individuals, and what's of interest to one child may not necessarily interest another, and that's okay. We have to love them for who they are and take the good with the not so good.

14

Motherhood

What can I say about the joys of becoming a mum, except 'lost identity': *Who are you?*

Am I no longer the free, fun-loving person I used to be? As my kids so kindly put it, I'm cranky and I'm always cleaning. All I ever seem to hear is: 'When can we go to the dam?' 'When can we go to the skate park?' 'When can we go?'

It doesn't matter to them that my laundry resembles a nuclear bombsite and not one but two Chinese laundromats rolled together, and that I can't keep up with the incessant folding of laundry. James, in his wisdom, tells me 'to fold as I go'. It sounds great in theory, and I'm sure there are many women out there who are way more organised than me, and pedantically fold as they go. They are most likely Virgos.

I might add that I don't see my husband picking up any clothes to fold. Men. All talk and no action.

Actually, that's the story of my life when it comes to James. He's always so full of advice and suggestions, none of which he actually puts into practice himself.

I'm a multi-personality Gemini myself, and I have the horrendous tendency of starting chores in one room, and becoming side-tracked and starting again in another room, meaning I end up with three or four rooms on the go at once.

We love our children dearly and wouldn't change our decision to have our family, but it's the most exhausting career path we will ever take in our lives. It involves so much for me over the course of a day. I'm a mother, carer, counsellor, mediator, referee, chef, cleaner, nurse (which, thankfully, I am), money machine, teacher and accountant. If James had to pay for all those services, he couldn't afford it.

Wives are expected to cope with anything the universe throws at them, just for the love of it all, while the husbands swan off to work and go about their usual activities. Not a lot changes for men when they marry and have a family, unless we marry a SNAG (sensitive new age guy), which I did not. I must add that James is not a chauvinist, but at the same time he doesn't care who does the work around the house as long as it's not him.

Trust me; there's never a dull moment in our household. We have four kids. The fourth child made no difference to my workload, except for maybe an extra load of washing a day. Once you have the third one, what's one more? Perhaps some people develop the attitude that once they have four kids, what's another three or four to come over and play? It really makes no difference. Sometimes it actually makes life easier to have other kids over, as then my own aren't constantly pestering me with the constant 'can we go' mantra. So that gives me more time to keep on cleaning.

Jean is still single and sends me texts, saying: *What you doin?* I'll text back: *Cleaning.* Two hours later I'll get another text from her: *What you doin?* Again, I'll text back: *Cleaning.* What does she think I'm doing, with four kids at heel? Relaxing on a tropical island sipping cocktails? In my dreams. I would be throwing back Pina Coladas, except I'm bit lactose sensitive so that might not go down too well.

Another frustrating, classic example of kids and their constant demands is when I'm on the phone and I'm in the middle of a full-blown conversation. I can bet a million dollars that a child will come up and ask a question. If I mouth 'I'm on the phone', do they listen? No.

Then they start tapping my shoulder chanting, 'Mummy, Mummy, Mummy.' By then I'm making so many hand signals that I could land a jumbo jet on an international runway, but they still persist.

I'll cover the receiver and threaten them with near death; tell them they're rude, ignorant children and unless there's blood pouring out of someone, or a limb is hanging off someone's body, or a major house fire has broken out, then it's not important enough for them to interrupt me.

It's always especially exasperating when I've been on the line to Telstra for hours, hours and more hours. Do my kids come and speak to me when I'm on hold? Never. They time it for the exact moment the operator speaks, when I have to politely excuse myself, explain I have four kids, hoping they'll take pity on me, and that I just have to see to one of those ill-mannered darlings.

Thomas took sleeping with us to a whole new level. I woke up one morning stinking of urine. I'd forgotten to put a nappy on him before he went to bed and he had come in and climbed into bed with us. At some point he peed. With me being dead to the world I didn't notice he had just wet his pyjamas, part of my pillow and also my hair. OMG, that was a first: getting wet on in bed, and my hair.

Henry peed on my head when I first brought him home from hospital. I wasn't used to little boys with their deadly little weapon and still hadn't realised that if I didn't get a nappy back on him quick smart, I'd be christened all over again. I was in the nursery changing him and bent down to grab something off the bottom of the change table. All of a sudden I felt a trickle on my head. It was Henry, shooting to the skies, but it didn't land in the skies but on my head.

A woman's lot in life is to be a good person, to lead her children by example. Do we all place high expectations on ourselves? I know I do. I love being a mother, but it's a full-time job and completely exhausting at times, especially if you want to work as well and have other interests.

I've developed the art of multitasking. For example, at the moment I'm sitting in the car in front of the school madly trying to complete some last-minute details of this book so I can get it to my friend to read and then off to the editor next week. I know that once school ends for the day I won't get near it until after everyone goes to bed, and the weekend's out because tomorrow we're travelling five hours one way for cricket trials. The kids' homework always comes first, so it's homework, swimming and scouts this afternoon.

I wish I could be more disciplined and achieve more than I do with my hours, but when I'm at home I get sidetracked with house chores. I have office work to do, my shop, secretary stuff to catch up on, household finances—and my book, the least important of the everyday needs of a household with children and a husband.

I think it's great to show your children that you can try and do it all, but at what cost? Something has to give. James says I'm spread too thin and I'm not really achieving one hundred percent with anything. I'm inclined to agree, but once again it comes back to the high expectations I place on myself to be able to do it all. But *am* I doing it all?

Pride is an amazing feeling, especially with your kids. When Henry was selected for soccer trials, he tried but failed to prevent a smile bursting out on his face as wide as the Grand Canyon. And me? Well, I phoned James and started crying. Henry had tried out for cricket and rugby league, and both had been a no-go. He came away feeling deflated and a failure, and it didn't matter what I said or did, I couldn't pick him up to feel good about himself.

They had just finished the trial game for soccer when he started to get down in the dumps again.

'Come on, Mum,' he said, 'let's go. I'm not going to get picked.'

I told him to wait and see. Then his name was called out and it was music to my ears.

I had had to drive the three-hour round trip to a nearby town for him to try out for soccer, but it was worth it, whether he got selected or not. It's something I would always do, but to see his smile was a very special moment. That pride as a parent for a child's achievement is an amazing feeling. If I had been unable to take him to the trials, James would have had to do it. Being selected is so important for a child, and they need to have a parent there to share in their joy, or give them a big hug and tell them how great they are.

I didn't get on Facebook and advertise it to the world, although all my friends and family got a text from a very proud and excited mum.

Another thing that I find beautiful is when our children play together nicely. I love looking outside and seeing them hanging out and playing together, as usually my little darlings are trying to tear each other's throats out. Within a two-hour timeframe of getting home from school some days, they will have scuffed each other up at least three times, and when Ann cries it is like a poddy calf bellowing. She likes to let you know of any injustice, even though most times she instigates the first round.

I so rarely get any me-time. One day I had dinner sorted and had just finished doing some homework with them they were playing out the back, so I thought I would grab a wine and sit on the front step and enjoy the tranquillity of the afternoon. Not with my lot. They instinctively know when I'm trying to have some chill time, and before I could blink they were out the front, arguing over some injustice in the game they were playing. That was the end of wine-o'clock for me.

Once I just needed to have time out so I climbed up into their wooden cubbyhouse out the back with a wee drop of wine in tow and sat there with my phone, catching up with my friend Donna, who was beside herself laughing at me hiding out in the kid's cubbyhouse. Picture a grown woman hiding in a cubbyhouse, guzzling her one glass of wine. The only mistake I made was not to take the bottle.

Donna just loves the madness of my kids, so I'm glad I can be a source of entertainment for her. She carries on about how mad the kids are, but most of the time she's encouraging their madness, with me looking like the serious ogre trying to bring order to the insanity of it all. Sometimes I don't bother. I just switch off to another personality and look at them vaguely, like I'm standing from the outside looking in. I quite often get asked, 'Are you listening?' I often feel like replying that I'm not, but if I'm told something worth listening to, it just might grab my attention.

Some days seem like ground-hog day; same shit, different day. It's a bit hard to focus when they all want a piece of you. Once I did actually tell them to let me cut myself in three, so I could attend to each of their ever so demanding requests.

What I've learned from motherhood is that it's a privilege, and is not to be taken lightly. We're responsible for shaping those tiny little beings into responsible adults, and the old adage 'monkey see, monkey do' is spot on. I realise how fortunate I am, that not every mother has the privilege of dropping everything to attend their kids' school activities or sporting functions. They have to work full time as well. James has given me the opportunity to be the mother I want to be and supports everything else I choose to do.

What I've learned about motherhood is to show my children that it may just be possible to achieve their goals as well as be a good parent. Only time will tell.

15

Brawling Kids

A couple of years ago we went to Townsville to our friend's fortieth birthday party. We were out the backyard enjoying the festivities when James and I heard the noise of kids fighting. A couple of adults come over to us and asked us if they should intervene.

On closer inspection, and much to our embarrassment, we saw that it was our two older kids fighting. Of course. At least Henry and Ann don't fail to disappoint us. They'll either get along together beautifully and play together really well, or fight and antagonise each other ruthlessly.

When they both did swimming they had to be placed in different lanes, and at tennis they were put into different groups. James says they have to work it out between them, and, really, if Henry wanted to he could put Ann down, but he knows he's not allowed to punch girls. I feel sorry for him when she picks up anything within in reach and attacks him.

One afternoon the kids were outside playing, and James and I were watching them from the kitchen. Ann was in a mood and wanted to fight Henry, and he was displaying his tendency to say things to aggravate her. We could see that Henry didn't want to physically fight her, so he was avoiding that at all costs, but his Achilles heel is his brothers, especially William. Ann knows that, and she attacked William for no reason except to upset Henry.

There were bodies scattered as they got at it tooth and nail. To our horror, Henry sank the boot into a fallen Ann. We could see her hand coming free, feeling for whatever she could to lay him out with, but then he peed on her. OMG, we couldn't believe what we were seeing.

James launched off the veranda, and the big kids scattered to the four winds. He was after them, but now they joined forces against their father.

All I can say is thank the Lord we have fourteen acres of land around our home, as we're certainly not fit to be living next to civilised people. I'm sure psychologists would have a field day analysing my little darlings, but I've resigned myself to the diagnosis that they are feral. That night Henry and Ann were the best of buddies again.

Never a dull moment.

That story is just one of many, and when we visit people or we go out in public I threaten the kids with near death if they embarrass me in front of people. I'm going to relish the time when I can share some of these moments of madness at each of their twenty-firsts.

I have three boys and one girl, and I'm terrified of them growing up in this day and age with all the drugs and other traps there are out there. We talk openly about the effects of drugs and making responsible choices in life. I do explain to them that there are always consequences for their actions, and they can choose the wrong path, but they have to be prepared to face the consequences. I've given much thought to the teenage years ahead. Ugh.

Some of my friends think I'm nuts, but I've said that I'm going to take them to a homeless shelter for drug addicts and troubled youth so they can see first-hand what choices some people have made and the consequences that follow. There's nothing like seeing and speaking to such people first-hand, and if that doesn't work and they still make the wrong choices, I can't say I didn't try.

As a nurse, I see people from all walks of life coming to the hospital for sharps kits, a container with needles and a syringe that is intended to prevent needle sharing. And as I also live in a small town, and it can be quite uncomfortable and confronting to see those people in the street the next day. I was dealing with one such person at work one day who asked me how my kids were doing as I was handing over the sharps kit. Not much makes me uncomfortable as a nurse, but that was up there with the best.

What I've learned about kids and fighting is to leave them to sort out their own battles. If that fails, the next best thing is to crack open a bottle of wine and go hide in the car or cubbyhouse. Or call a friend and pretend your kids aren't yours. Imagine there was a mix-up at the hospital and your own well-behaved little darlings are going to turn up any minute.

16

Kids and Shopping

I sent Henry into the shop one day with his younger siblings for some chips and gravy. It's their usual Friday afternoon treat, after a torturous week of homework and school. He came back out to the car exasperated by the behaviour of his brothers and sisters. One was climbing on something, another one was touching the glass with the cooked chips, and another said something to his mate's friend that embarrassed him. *Now* Henry understands why I don't want to go shopping with all of them in tow.

Before my children were born, when I used to see other people's little gremlins running through the supermarket or other shops, climbing all over everything, I used to idly wonder why the mother couldn't control her children. They're so naughty, I would think. I wouldn't put up with that. In the

16 KIDS AND SHOPPING

distant background of this mayhem I would hear a voice saying, 'Stop that. Come back here.' It knew it was just a background hum that the little darlings would pay no attention to.

Then it happened to *me* one day. I was in Woolworths doing the shopping, minding my own business, when I noticed something fly past me. I realised it was one of my children racing past, being chased by their brother. Then I happened to look down and there were the same speed racers doing commando rolls under the dividing aisles. I was *so* embarrassed.

I said in a firm but quiet voice, using the mummy tone, 'Stop that right now.'

There was an employee nearby, packing shelves. Well, the poor woman stopped what she was doing and looked at me in horror. How embarrassing. I had to explain that I didn't mean her but my errant children, who were rolling from aisle to aisle.

The woman had heard and taken notice of my remarks, but do you think those out-of-control gremlins did? Oh, no. They continued their assault on the supermarket and I knew with full certainty that there was a single person hovering in the background somewhere, thinking: Why can't that woman control her children?

It gets even better. We got to the checkout and I looked over to where one child was riding the brown guide-dog figurine and another was climbing the Everest-sized display of potting mix. I've never been so grateful to leave the supermarket in all my life.

Now, unless it's for reasons beyond my control, I

do not take them to the supermarket together. I will take one or two but never the four together.

Kmart is different. I can manage taking them there because it's a very large shop and when they run around there, to a certain extent I can pretend they aren't mine. They just go from one toy aisle to another, most of the time, although on occasion I've looked around and found them swinging through the clothes racks.

I've looked around at other times to see Henry and Ann in a full-blown brawl. There's no other way of describing it. They will scratch, punch or kick simply because Ann has a hot head. Her fuse is *so* short. Henry only has to say something, or bump her, and it's all on. Oscar de la Hoya would be hard pressed to break up those two when they get started. It's hard for Henry, who knows he's not to hit girls, so he tries other self-defence mechanisms to protect himself from his crazed sister.

I just keep walking, and unless they sing out 'Mum' no one knows they're mine.

When at Kmart I need to lay down the rules upon entering. They can get only one toy each, costing no more than ten dollars. Failure to set out the rules can result in me spending the entire time saying 'No!' to the point that I need one of those little pocket tape recorders so I can just keep pressing play and have it repeat 'No!' over and over and over.

There's always one who feels they've been treated unjustly and life is unfair and their sibling's toy is fifty cents more than the one they have. I've tried the whole 'there are starving kids on the other side of the world that would be grateful for anything they were given'

16 KIDS AND SHOPPING

ploy, but it's a waste of time. They don't listen. If it doesn't revolve around them, it doesn't exist.

If this book sells, I think I might plan a trip to some underprivileged country so I can show these little darlings of mine another way of living. Then and only then would I have any hope that it would penetrate their skulls to realise how fortunate they are.

I'm not sure what people think about child harnesses and wrist leads on kids, but I found them an essential item when we were travelling overseas. The bigger kids wore wrist leads, but the youngest had a body harness and would throw herself down like a mad bull calf when we went to put it on her.

We were travelling in Singapore and as we were going shopping in the markets and down to the mall among such a lot of people, it was very easy for a small child to get lost. Little Joyce would actually get her wrist lead for me to put on her, which was quite cute. Apparently I used to do the same with my mother. Megan, on the other hand, would throw a tantrum over her harness, the same as my daughter did, and I hope that's where their similarities end.

The one moment we didn't put on the kids' leads was when we had just arrived at Singapore airport and were busily bundling everyone out of the car into the terminal. We did a head count and found one down. Henry wasn't anywhere to be seen. For ten minutes we were frantic. I stayed with the other kids while James went looking for him and thankfully found him daydreaming and ambling along. Nothing has changed. To this day he still dawdles along in his own little world.

Singapore airport is not a great place to lose your child. At times like that the mind goes into overdrive. We felt like screaming, 'We have no money so don't even *think* of ransom,' but I think that would have looked a little extreme.

What I've learned about kids and shopping is that they don't mix. If at all possible, don't take them. Will it really matter much if they grow up having never seen the inside of a supermarket?

17

Road Trips with Kids

I've never thought I couldn't just jump in the car and go. Having four kids has never held me back in that regard. I've done a lot of road trips with my kids and a couple of plane flights, usually by myself because James is always working.

By the time he was four months old, Henry had been to Melbourne, when James had his ankle replacement done. When Henry was ten months old, Constance and I went to Darwin for a two-week uni block for our nursing degree. It was a twenty-hour drive and overall Henry coped very well.

Before I had children of my own I used to take my niece Joyce on holidays with me. I remember travelling to Brisbane to see my cousin before she left to go to England for work. We travelled as far as my grandmother's farm, which was about forty-five minutes from Rockhampton, and then went on to Brisbane the next day.

Joyce didn't cope well with the car trip. She was two years old and decided to scream all the way from Cabarita to Gin Gin, or maybe Childers, one of those little towns. This is nuts, I thought, I'll end up having a car accident. I pulled up at the nearest pharmacy and got some Phenergan. It's a marvellous drug used for allergic skin reactions, nausea and vomiting, but also *sedation*, so I gave Joyce a dose as per the guidelines and my darling niece relaxed and slept for the remainder of the journey to Brisbane.

On our return trip, I didn't have to give her any sedation; she was a dream child. She must have thought, I'd better behave or I'm going to be sleeping again. Joyce is a lot like me and hates to miss out on anything.

Jean travelled with me by car from Brisbane to Sale in Victoria. Megan was living there at the time and we were going down to visit and also bring Joyce, who was five, back home with us. I took Henry, who was two.

It took a couple of days to drive from Queensland to Victoria and back. I discovered that Joyce has inherited my disorder of being able to talk, talk, talk. My family would always tease me when I was a child, telling me that I could talk underwater.

We hadn't even left Victoria when I looked in the rear-vision mirror, and there was Henry with a plastic bucket on his head. I couldn't see his face and that was his point. Joyce had talked so much that, even at the age of two, Henry was exhausted and must have thought, if she can't see my head she might be quiet just for a minute.

Joyce finally gave up and fell asleep, and I thought Henry was sleeping too, until I saw a little hand slowly and stealthily reach to a position in the door cavity where he had been hoarding some chicken nuggets. He grabbed the nuggets and very quietly snuck them up inside the bucket and into his mouth, obviously in fear that if he made too much noise he might wake his beautiful chatterbox cousin sitting next to him. Henry adored Joyce, but even his adoration for his cousin was diminished by the fact that she had just plain wore the little man out.

I'm sure others have had a screaming baby in the car and been unable to pull over. We just have to keep driving and hope for the best that at some point they'll admit defeat. We all know that usually doesn't happen. Babies have the stamina of endurance riders.

On one particular occasion, I was travelling with Joyce again, who was five, Henry, who was two, and Ann, who was eight months. We had just been on holiday to visit my Grandma at her farm and were on our way back, but we broke the trip with a stopover with relatives in Barcaldine.

Miss Ann decided to scream her head off for the last hour of the journey, and I started weighing up my options. Should I pull over and see if she was hungry, which I thought was highly unlikely as I had only fed her at our stop in Emerald, or keep going and hope that she would stop?

Well, poor Joyce was beside herself. 'Aunty Tara, please make her stop. I have a headache.'

I felt for her. Ann had and still has a bellow of a Brahman bull. Henry, bless him, had fallen asleep in all the commotion. Finally we got to Barcaldine at nine pm and

I felt for my relatives to be turning up very late, with one very persistent, screaming child. The little darling stopped the minute the car stopped and we got out. She stopped screaming and behaved like a child sent from heaven, so the entire ordeal was a temper tantrum. She was obviously sick of car travelling and thought she would share her annoyance and make everyone else's life a living hell.

Travelling with kids *and* being pregnant is never much fun either. When I was twenty weeks pregnant with Thomas, I had to make the trek to Cabarita with Henry, Ann and William because my grandmother was in hospital dying of cancer and she wanted to die at home. As nurses, my mum and I decided to get there as quickly as we could so we could take her home to the farm. I travelled from home straight through the Tuesday night. It was a thirteen-hour trip.

We went into Rockhampton the next day and arranged for an ambulance to bring her home. She got home on Wednesday and died on the Thursday. It was sad, as we had hoped to have a little more time with her, but as a nurse I knew when we got her home that she would not see the week out in her frail condition.

It had been a couple of emotionally exhausting days, so on the weekend my mum, Louise and one of our cousins decided to take the kids to Yeppoon for the day, to get away from all the upset.

We were at Emu Park and I was down by the sea playing with the kids while my mother and my cousin were lying down under a shady tree having a nap. My mum heard a strange noise and someone talking to her and then felt something on her shoulder. At first she thought it was my cousin playing tricks on her, until she opened her eyes and there was a beautiful green parrot sitting on her shoulder, happily chatting away. It had taken a real shine to her.

We got in the car and went up to Emu Park police station, thinking someone might be there and we could turn him in. However, that was not to be the case, so instead we drove all the way back to Rockhampton with a pet. When we eventually got home I was travelling with three kids under six, a parrot and a puppy.

It was definitely a wild drive home. I was twenty weeks pregnant and wetting myself every time I coughed. Even when I went to the funeral I thought I was going to have to succumb to granny pads and pants. So embarrassing. And I had to keep pulling over to vomit on the way down. It was not my best road trip.

The road trip I did with the kids to have Thomas was a long one, but first I need to paint a picture of life before we left. We had just finished building our new house and had to move from our family home into the new one. I never think that I can't get something done, so, as always, there I was, nearly full term, lifting and packing up our stuff. We moved in two days, over the May Day weekend.

The following week I had to clean our old house, as tenants were moving into it. With the help of my mother and two friends, I cleaned for nearly three nights straight, from seven-thirty pm to midnight. Meanwhile I still had to do all the normal routine chores at the new house. *Sadie, the cleaning lady ...*

I would get home about midnight and finish doing things before hitting the pillow at one am. Then I was up again at six am to get the kids off to school. This madness went on for a week.

Then I had to get ready to drive off into the sunrise to have Thomas, which meant packing for me and the other three kids. James would not be flying down to Townsville until the following Thursday. Saturday morning arrived, and the kids and I finally got away by about nine am. James was getting excited at the thought of having the house to himself and sneaking off to the races.

Well, I can safely say it was a *long* trip. I had to keep repositioning myself as I drove; I was getting a lot of cramping and felt very uncomfortable.

We finally arrived in Charters Towers to collect my mother in-law, who was coming to Townsville to stay with me until James arrived. We got to the units on The Strand at eight pm and went to bed.

The next day I stupidly took the kids to The Strand for a walk and then down to the waterpark, walking the entire distance. Why was there no one around strong enough to tell me to rest?

We went shopping at Target the next day as I had things I needed to buy for the kids. I had my week all mapped out—lunch with a friend; have a massage, and so on—but while at Target I knew things would not be going to plan. Envision an overstuffed, beached whale cramping on the floor of Target. I don't have small babies. They were all close to ten pounds, so I was a size to say the least.

No, *no*, this could not be happening, I thought. I'm not one for making a spectacle of myself, so I got my shit together and finished shopping. Then I got a phone call from Aunty Bella. She and her daughter Leith had flown from Brisbane to Townsville to surprise me, which was the most wonderful news, and I felt the need to push myself some more so I could hang out with them.

We walked on The Strand, chatting and hanging out, and I didn't mention I was having tightenings and cramping. That night I insisted on going to the fish and chip shop and getting dinner. OMG. I placed the order, walked over to the bottle shop and bought a bottle of wine. As I put it in the car I doubled over in pain. I did some serious controlled breathing, using all my willpower to keep my shit together, and wobbled back across the road to grab the food.

It's well known that nurses make the worst kind of patient, and I was booked into the hospital to have a caesarean delivery on the following Monday.

I got back to the unit, served up the meal, and had a wonderful time hanging out with rellies. In a moment of madness, I left the kids with my mother-in-law and went down to Aunty Bella's room to watch *Brothers and Sisters*. I got back to my unit about ten pm, and had barely got in the door when William, who was nearly two, had a croup attack. I gave him his Prednisolone medication, calmed him down, and realised that my contractions were coming nearly five minutes apart.

I took some Panadeine Forte tablets, which didn't have much effect on my pain at all. I woke my mother-in-law and asked if she had anything stronger. Did I really think she would have a spare Pethidine injection in her bag? And with my needle phobia, I would hardly have given myself a shot, even if she did have. She got up in a panic and we decided that she would sit up with William while Aunty Bella took me to the hospital.

We jumped in the car and off we went. While I drove we discussed the quickest route to the hospital.

Should I go to the hospital I was booked into, or to the general hospital emergency department? We phoned the after-hour numbers and went to the maternity ward, where someone buzzed us in. I had them convinced that I had a urinary-tract infection and if they just gave me some antibiotics to nip this whole labour thing in the bud, I could go about my business as planned.

They gave me a Pethidine injection for the pain and I phoned James at six am. He drove home from work in a panic, where a friend met him, helped him pack and got him on the road. I kept telling everyone I refused to have the baby until my husband arrived. At eight-thirty am I was sent home with a course of oral antibiotics and Panadol. Like Panadol was going to help. Aunty Bella drove me back to the hotel unit via a pharmacy, where I bought some Merysndol.

One of my best mates is a midwife in Townsville. When she came to visit me I asked her, 'If I just about overdose on these antibiotics do you think it will stop the contractions?'

I'm still amazed that the hospital let me go home, actively contracting, with the full knowledge it was to be my fourth caesarean birth. Henry had been an emergency Caesarean delivery and weighed a healthy 10 pounds 5 ounces, and they didn't even let me do a trial labour with the second child. My medical history showed clearly that my babies were not going to be delivered via the passage nature had intended.

After many antibiotic capsules, James arrived at about two-thirty pm. He had driven straight to the hospital, expecting me to be there, but was told I was back at the hotel unit. I was still trying to talk everyone around to the idea that it was not happening and *now* I rest. How stupid of me.

At seven pm, after multiple warm showers, James took me back to the hospital. By that stage things were in full swing. I managed to hold it all together until Aunty Bella walked in. Then the tears flowed, and those who know me well know I don't make a habit of crying in public. Because Aunty Bella is my dad's youngest sister, she is the person who most closely connects me to my dad, so she let me be a big sook.

I was so unimpressed with this baby. How dare it ruin all my plans? I had everything organised and, as I can be a control freak, I wasn't coping.

When Thomas was born at about ten pm and I saw my beautiful baby boy, I got over my hang-ups of my plans being foiled by him being in a hurry to enter the world. There was my little bully Taurus, who was born in the year of the ox. A double bull, God help us.

Not long ago, the whole family was in Townsville again as James needed an operation. He had a lot of blood tests, so while this was happening I took the kids to see a Lego display at the art gallery. We were in the car on our way back to pick him up when William announced he was feeling sick in the belly.

I was a bit casual. 'We won't be long. We'll just pick up Dad and take him back to the hotel for a rest.'

But it was not to be. James got in the car, and we were navigating a roundabout when William started vomiting. Henry, who was sitting next to him, shoved a blanket under William's face for him to vomit into. Then I heard the sound of Thomas vomiting in sympathy. Poor Henry was stuck between these two heaving boys.

We came out of the roundabout with James yelling, 'Stop the car!'

I pulled into the bike lane and he jumped out of the car like a gazelle being hunted. Thank goodness we had some water in the car so I could clean up the boys and make things tolerable. I don't know what people thought as they drove past. A bunch of hillbillies had hit the big smoke, maybe?

On this same trip to Townsville I took the kids to the beach to wear them out. There were some guys swimming near the kids, and one of them lost his sunglasses in the water. They washed up onto the beach near Thomas and I asked Thomas to give them to the man, which he did. The man said, 'Thanks, bro,' in a kindly manner.

Thomas informed me, and everyone else within a one-kilometre radius, that 'the black man just called me bro'. Henry wanted the surf to swallow him up. I sat there thinking, please let me sink into the sand and hide. The man heard him, as did everyone else in close proximity.

The things that come out of little boys' mouths can be too embarrassing for words. I actually get a bit nervous sometimes when I hear them start to comment on something.

What I've learned from road trips and kids is to never leave home without portable DVD players, and/or iPads, and have them fully stocked with movies. And when all else fails, on your arrival use alcohol to drown your sorrows.

18

Housework

Housework. Why do we have to do it? I wish at times that I were a slob so I wouldn't get so obsessed with cleaning. As a child, I kept my room spotless. Everything had its place. My sister's room was just the opposite. Let's just say that even rodents were afraid to enter in case they caught something. But now that I have four kids and a husband, it takes a lot more time and effort to keep on top of the household cleaning.

I keep the basics clean, and then on school holidays I try to do inside the cupboards. In the meantime, if I can shut the cupboard door, I can pretend its interior is neat, unless, of course, we have to open that door, which can often be a health and safety hazard.

I recently realised that I've been cleaning bathrooms and dusting since I was nine years old. After my mother left I became responsible for cleaning the house.

I think it's important for kids to learn to clean, so I do get them to help me at times, to sweep, mop and dust, especially in their own rooms. They have even cleaned the bathroom. But I don't want them to have to do too much, especially Ann, as odds are as a female she'll do way more housework than any of her brothers, but she still has to know how to clean.

Ann's room can look like a bombsite. At times there are empty bottles shoved into drawers, and dirty clothes jammed into the toybox with the dolls' clothes. Most times her room smells stale, as though everything in it could do with a good bath.

On the weekends when I work at the hospital, the house is chaos. There are many words to describe the mess. A long time ago I gave up tidying when I got home from work on the Saturday, as it would be in the same state of disarray on the Sunday. One time when I came home I was so mad that I lost it. I packed up all the cups, bowls and cutlery, and just left out the exact amount needed for each person. It worked for a while but then gradually the packed-away items returned. I decided to save my breath, and my stress levels, and switch off, as no one was listening to my ranting anyhow.

It was one of those moments where I had to decide to pick the battles I could win. And this was not one of them. So now I just exist with the chaos around me on those weekends and clean up on Monday.

What I've learned about housework is that what doesn't get done today can be done tomorrow. I do what I can , and am thankful I *have* a house to clean, and a happy, healthy family to share it with.

19

Cooking

'Mum, I'm hungry, what's for tea? Toasted grass, or bread and pull it?'

I can remember as a child pestering my father about what was for tea, and now my children do it to me.

When Dad said 'bread and pull it' I used to think it was some kind of stew. It wasn't until I was an adult that I understood what he was saying, or the meaning behind it. Jean uses the words 'toasted grass', which the kids didn't understand at first. Now they've worked out—a lot quicker than I did—that it means 'stop asking and we'll tell you when dinner is ready'.

I've reached the conclusion that I just need to keep meals simple and as healthy as I can make it for the kids. They don't require or desire anything fancy. My kids have always loved green veggies and salads, so it's pretty much a guarantee that they'll have 'green trees' or 'white tree' (broccoli or cauliflower) on their plate, and of course the universal mashed potatoes.

Their taste buds are starting to develop. Ann will be daring and have corn, pumpkin and sweet potatoes, although the boys are still stuck on trees. She will also have avocado, beetroot and asparagus, but once again the boys are stuck on the basics. Salads consist of lettuce, carrot, sliced apple and cheese. None of my kids have ever been interested in tomatoes and I love them.

As for fruit, again we keep it simple. The main fruit is apples, although over the last few years William has developed a taste for citrus fruits. Henry liked bananas when he was a toddler and I could never have enough lady-finger bananas. One day he ate seven bananas, and when I said he couldn't have anymore he started banging his head against the fridge.

I couldn't believe my eyes. I mentioned it to my mother, who mentioned it to the child-health nurse at her hospital, who wondered whether excess potassium from the bananas had sent Henry a bit troppo, like elderly people when they have a urinary tract infection and you think they're starting to lose it but then when you investigate further discover it's a simple electrolyte imbalance.

One day James came in and looked at the small round lumps on the kitchen table and floor. 'What are those rocks doing on the table? Did one of the little kids bring them in?'

I knew exactly what they were but I dared not say anything. The last time he caught my pet goat Annabelle on the kitchen table eating the leftover breakfast dishes he promptly gave her a choking and threw her out the door.

In a calm, beige voice, I lied. 'The kids were eating small boxes of sultanas.' Narrowly averting the madness that could have erupted, I swiftly cleaned up all evidence of my beautiful goat's droppings.

I love cookbooks and have a huge collection, but when I use a recipe for the first time I'm very anal about sticking to it rigidly. I don't add anything or take anything out until I've tasted it for the first time. Then I think, okay, I can add this or leave this out next time.

It drives Jean nuts; she likes to think she's Nigella Lawson. She and her mother used to pretend they were interviewing each other for a cooking show. Jean now does it with me, and whether I can get into the groove or not depends on what mood I'm in. Also, if she and I are in the kitchen cooking together it can become quite tense, as she's always looking over my shoulder.

When I say, 'What?' she will say, 'Nothing,' but I just know she wants to say *something*. Depending on whether I'm calm or am having an eye-bulging moment, she knows whether or not to interfere.

If James is a typical example, when husbands cook they use every pot in the house and clean up nothing. I remember once before we had kids, when we were living together, I couldn't find my roasting dish. Then one day I went down the back of our flat for something and there was my dish, hiding among the trees where he had left it soaking for weeks. It was a dish of rust.

Kids can crush my efforts in the kitchen by saying, 'I don't like this.' Or they'll tell me that so-and-so cooks it much better. Lucky for me, I don't get compared to their grandmothers' cooking, as neither my mother nor my husband's mother is a cook.

One night I served up dinner on the veranda. William was late to the table as usual. The next minute I had a tearful four year old crying at my heels, telling me that Tiger, our pet cat, had been eating off his plate.

In my exhausted beige moment, I said, 'It's okay, mate, he wouldn't have eaten much. I just fed him.'

Who knows why the other kids didn't shoo Tiger away. He's lucky I didn't catch him, as he would have been spear-tackled off the veranda.

I used to love cooking once and was very adventurous, always cooking with a glass of wine close at hand, but with the pressures of kids' taste buds and homework, meals have become simple although still tasty. Only in the last few years has Henry been willing to have mince with the spaghetti bolognaise; Ann stills eats only the meat and not the pasta.

What I've learned about cooking is to keep it simple and nutritious. I try to cook meals that cater to everyone's taste buds. Failing that, they can have an apple for tea, as I don't cook different meals for each child.

20

Homework

Who was it that invented homework, I wonder. Obviously it was someone single, who didn't have to come home to a bunch of kids. I'm not teacher material. Many a time a child in our house has been hit on the head with a reading book.

When I'm reading with them there's nothing that frustrates me more than when they can't remember the very word they just said two lines ago, and have been told ten times already. Then the guessing starts as they sound out a letter that's totally different letter to the one that the word actually starts with. Then they look at me like I'm stupid for correcting them. OMG, where's the wine?

As I sit here typing, Ann is doing her homework and periodically throwing her pencil across the room in fits of temper as I chastise her for messy handwriting. Once again, what brainiac thought homework was a good thing? Kids go to school all day and then come home and spend another hour doing homework.

Being a conscientious parent, it takes me nearly an hour every afternoon to help the kids with their homework. I could just chill, drink a bottle of wine and let them fend for themselves (it crosses my mind). Is all this fighting worth it? Are they going to be geniuses and bring about world peace?' Highly unlikely.

I'm doing battle with Ann, trying to extend her vocabulary beyond a one-line sentence. She, in turn, has no qualms about arguing with me that one line is a long sentence. She accuses me of picking on her and asks what my problem is.

Henry cries and becomes emotional when I ask if he's done his homework. Thankfully, after ripping out his homework pages, he does do neat work now, which has been a miracle in itself.

The times tables are a whole different story. In my day we parrot-learned our times tables, and we remembered them. Now they teach them completely differently and, surprise, surprise, Henry still doesn't know his times tables. According to him, my way is not how it's done. 'We don't do it like that,' he says.

Does this sound familiar ? They may not do it like that anymore, but guess who knows their tables and who doesn't.

William is doing homework now, but thankfully doesn't give me any grief. Thomas, is in prep and about to start homework, which could also be interesting.

What I've learned about kids and homework is to keep the wine handy. It's a necessary tool for homework (for the parent).

21

Bathtime

I don't know whether I'm not strict enough or if it's just what happens in my bathroom, but it can look like an indoor pool by the time the kids finish having a bath some days, with clothes scattered everywhere and a lake of water that would have our ducks excited.

I've introduced a new rule: if they don't pick up their clothes and place them in the basket, I'm not washing them. But I have to remind them every day, and with four kids, the clothes just pile up if I don't wash at least two loads every day.

When I remember, I also get them to clean their own bathroom. The dirt that comes off the kids and leaves a ring around the bath, like in *The Cat in the Hat*, is ridiculous. Sometimes I'm sure they've brought the grime of the whole garden in with them when they come inside.

In winter I put olive oil in the bath water to help keep their skin from drying out, especially as we're on our own bore-water supply. This doesn't help with the dirt scenario. Instead it just makes it stick to the sides even more.

I gave up letting them use cakes of soap years ago, as they would just leave the soap sitting in the water, and within a day one cake of soap would have become soap custard. So now I use liquid soap, but I can't even leave that in there as they'll pour the entire bottle in and create a lake of suds instead.

Henry and Ann are the worst. I've taken to buying cheap bubble bath, as baths have become too costly. I keep the good stuff in my room, and take it into their bathroom and pour it in myself, plus some Dettol. Who knows what germs they can pick up outside, so I throw a splash of that into the tub for good measure.

What I've learned about bathtime is to try to save my dollars by using cheap bath liquid. And kids don't know the difference between good-quality towels or lesser quality, so I go cheap.

22

Bedtime

I think I've heard just about every excuse there is for not going to bed at the allocated time, although there are probably many more out there.

I have a set bedtime for the kids, and try to stick to it, but putting four kids to bed every night can be quite a chore and sometimes their bedtimes go past the allotted hour.

I made the terrible mistake with Henry of lying down with him when putting him to sleep, and even now he sucks his fingers and needs to play with my hair. Ann needs to hold my hand. William sucks his thumb and plays with my hair. And Thomas likes me to play with his foot. So basically I have to split myself into four pieces, like an act in a magic show, to get them all to sleep.

Thomas recently came up with the excuse of being thirsty in a feeble attempt to get back out of his bed, to delay sleep for just a few more minutes, even though he'd had a drink before getting into bed. He insisted on me pinching his foot, and when I didn't pinch the bottom of his foot just right, he told me not to scratch but to pinch it. I can see him becoming either a dominatrix, or their submissive.

Henry came up with a good one, too. He wanted me to dig a prickle out of his foot. I pointed out to him that when he was playing on my laptop an hour earlier, the prickle hadn't bothered him, but he insisted it was so sore he couldn't sleep.

I'm getting bored with the whole prickle thing. If they just wore their shoes, they wouldn't have to get me to dig out prickles. For some strange reason, Henry enjoys it. When he was a little fellow I couldn't get anywhere near his feet until he went to sleep. OMG, I've never seen another person like it. Henry can sleep so deeply that we used to wait until he was asleep to dig out the prickles. James says that he wouldn't believe it if he hadn't seen it for himself.

To feel that all-encompassing, engulfing love, you have to wait until they go to sleep. I've always said that kids need to go to sleep to re-energise the love you have for them.

I've always found something spiritual and beautiful about sleeping people, especially children. I used to feel the same way about my sister Megan when we were young. She could be so horrible at times, then she would go to sleep. I'd go in and look at her, lying there looking so angelic. I used to wonder how someone who looked like that asleep could drive me so nuts when she was awake.

Kids push us to the limit sometimes, to the point where you need to back away before causing grievous bodily harm.

22 BEDTIME

My kids have the same effect on me. By the time I do the ground-hog day morning routine of getting up, getting the kids dressed for school, making breakfast and lunches, and then the afternoon routine of homework, dinner, baths and bed—all of which fight against every step of the way—it's a marvellous feeling when the last one closes their eyes and mouth and goes to sleep. Then I look at them, feeling totally exhausted, as though I've run the world's longest marathon, and that overwhelming feeling of love comes over me. They look so angelic and peaceful. I stand there thinking, yep, those little scallywags are mine and I wouldn't have it any other way.

What I've learned about bedtime is to try and use all my restraint, as the kids can push all my buttons and more. But once they're asleep and I look down at them, they just look like little angels and my love is reenergised for another day.

School Holidays

OMG, the dreaded sound of, 'I'm bored.' How often I hear that phrase over the school holidays. How many times do we hear ourselves sounding like our parents? I do, especially when the kids say they're bored. I've often found myself repeating, 'If you keep saying you're bored, I'm sure I can find something for you to do.' There's always something to be done in our household of six.

I love the school holidays. No homework, no school lunches, no school routines, and if I don't want to leave the house for a few days I don't have to. In winter it's so nice to sit in the lounge room with the kids, snuggled up under the blankets watching the cartoons on ABC2 or ABC3. The kids can stay in their pyjamas all day if they want to, and if I get caught up in cleaning or doing other jobs even I've been known to still be in my pyjamas come lunchtime.

I do try to get cupboards cleaned during the school holidays. In between the holidays it's just

23 SCHOOL HOLIDAYS

maintenance cleaning, and making sure cupboard doors stay closed so no one can see how many things keep getting jammed back into them. Many a time I've opened a cupboard door and all sorts of crap has come tumbling down around me. Rather than picking it up and organising the cupboard contents, I cram it back in as best I can—and wait for the next school holidays.

Plus, there's the never-ending dusting. Ann is very good at dusting the mantelpieces, and her speciality is cleaning the bookshelves. It takes her ages, as she dusts and rearranges the books as she sees fit, but no one's about to argue with that. If she didn't do it, it wouldn't get done until the next school holidays.

As a special holiday treat I usually take the kids to a nearby town to see a movie on cheap Tuesday. I can't remember the last time I saw an adult movie at the cinema—it's always the kids' ones. I always have my children with me, and it's not like I'm going to do a three-hour return trip while they're at school just to go see an adult flick.

I love the Oscars and watch them every year. I used to watch them with my dad. When the Oscar nominations are released every year, I've always seen every animation movie. One year I was watching the Oscars with Aunty Belly, and she was horrified that I knew all the animation contenders.

'You need to get a life,' she said. 'Spend some time on yourself.'

'Yeah, right, as if that's going to happen,' I said. 'It sounds good in theory, but my me-time days are when I can go to my wee shop, or head off to do some nursing at The Swamp.' The Swamp is a fond nickname some of us oldies have for the hospital.

I must admit I do feel a bit sorry for the kids at times, as I would be happy to stay home and catch up on jobs. Also to just not drive anywhere after all the running around I do when the kids are at school, but having a mortgage means going away for a holiday every school break is not a reality. Living in the Outback means we're hours away from holiday destinations. To fly anywhere is totally out of the question with a family of six, and it's an eight-hour drive to the nearest city.

James takes the kids fishing when he can, and they love camping, so I have to get on board with the whole camping scene so we can do that more often during our family holidays.

What I've learned about school holidays is to relax and make the most of them, as those years pass all too quickly.

24

School Mums

I'm sure there are mums out there like me who aren't apart of any cliquey group. Every morning I walk the gauntlet into school, being polite and saying hi to everyone I see, but I'm not invited or included to join anything the other women do.

At school, I help out as much as I can with reading groups. Every morning I help with William's reading group, and last year when he was in prep, every morning I did prep activity groups.

It's amazing, though. It's always the busy mums who end up helping the most with reading groups. The mums who have their coffee or exercise groups, or are in a rush to get home to Facebook, never seem to have enough time to help out in the mornings, but—shock, horror—they're the popular ones strutting their stuff, looking important.

I'm one of those polite mums who seem to know most people, but when I go to school functions I always feel out of place. James is usually too busy to come with me, so I usually tell the kids to hang out with me so I don't feel like a Noddy-no-friend.

In all honesty, I'm happy this way, as trying to run a shop, be the secretary for a local community group, work as a nurse, and be a mother and wife is enough.

What I've learned from facing the school-mum pack is to smile, say hello and just keep on walking.

25

Coffee Groups

James says it's because I don't do coffee mornings that our children are never invited anywhere to play with other kids, although that's been proven untrue lately, as they've definitely had a busy social calendar.

Once or twice a year I catch up with a select group of friends I made when I worked full time at the hospital. It's usually around our birthdays or Christmas time that we get together for lunch.

I just don't have enough time in my day to sit around chatting and having coffee. My life, like that of any mum who works outside the home and gives as much as possible to her children, is a rollercoaster ride that operates twenty-four hours a day without let-up.

Even at home in the mornings, I usually have my coffee on the go, and sometimes I don't even finish it as I'm busy making lunches and razzing kids to get ready.

I usually spend my time with Jean, as my other close friends are scattered throughout Queensland

and New South Wales. I do get together with another friend I once worked with, who also has children now, for coffee once a month.

A work colleague, who is also a friend, has small children, and her daughter and Thomas are the best of mates. Her daughter, although a year younger than my boy, has always been more advanced than my little fellow. It's so funny to watch them. She takes the lead and lets Thomas know what's happening, and whatever she decides to do, he's happy to go along with it.

My friend and I catch up for a coffee and play date about once a month. Apart from that, we see each other at school every day, and when we're busy with our respective reading groups, the little ones go in search of play and mischief.

What I've learned about socialising is to always treasure the moments when we do get to share that coffee or tea with a good mate, as there's no guarantee when the next one will be.

26

Relatives

You can pick your friends, but you're stuck with your relatives. But you need mad, deranged relatives because that's what *makes* a family. Who else can we talk with and laugh about at family gatherings? Families are interesting things, with loads of individual personalities.

The kids and I recently stayed at a self-contained unit at Cabarita Beach, south of Tweed Heads, for nine days while James was on a work course on the Gold Coast. I emailed my family and friends in Brisbane and told them where we were staying, if they would like to come and see us. I explained that I wouldn't be doing much driving, as I'd recently had a major abdominal operation.

Out of two uncles, three aunties and eight cousins that live in Brisbane, two aunts, one uncle and two cousins came to visit and it was great having that time with them, especially my cousins. We were all very close as children, and I'm still close to a couple of them.

It was an ideal opportunity for those who did come to spend time with my kids and get to know them. It was also great for my cousins and me, because when we were children we used to go to the same place with our parents, and now we were repeating history by taking our own children to holiday there.

I would love dearly for my cousins' kids and my kids to spend time with each other like we all used to when we were younger, but with me living in the bush and them in the city there are many constraints. Consequently we don't see my family as much as I would like.

I have fond memories of Christmases with my family. Every Christmas Dad would drive us to Aunty Bella's on the Sunshine Coast, a tradition that continued every year after my Grandma died, as before that everyone came home to her.

With life as it is, however, all the members of my family have grown apart and are now leading their own lives. I find that it's usually me who is the one trying to keep in touch, which can be hard. It's made me quite sad at times, but I know I can't change that; instead I just make the most of the relatives who do want to maintain a relationship.

What I've learned about family is to value the time you have with them. It's the quality of those individual moments that are important, not the quantity.

27

Family Holidays

Just recently we went to Cabarita Beach again for our holidays and stayed ten days in a self-contained unit. We flew down, picked up our new car and spent the night at the Gold Coast before driving down to Cabarita the next day.

In our wisdom we thought we would go to Wet'n'Wild on the Gold Coast on the way, and because we didn't want to be late of course we ended up there three hours early.

I stayed with two little ones, as I couldn't really do much after my recent operation, and off James went with Henry and Ann. They only managed to go on three rides in two hours. When everyone was back together I went on one gentle ride with the two big kids.

We announced that there would only be one more ride and then we had to get going, as we still had to collect our keys for the unit. Henry and Ann went missing in action and we couldn't find them. We just had to sit and wait for them to show up. Three hours later they came bouncing back, full of life. They'd been waiting in line to go down the slides and in that whole time had gone on only two rides, but they were happy, even though we were not.

Cabarita Beach has been a great find. When you cross the border into New South Wales, it's like stepping back in time and everything is affordable for families. Our unit backed straight onto the beach, which is gorgeous and without the usual crowds of people. We spent nearly six hours every day on the beach.

Coffee shops, boutiques and flash restaurants don't interest us when we're out with the kids; it's all about them. We've booked in for another holiday next year.

Family and friends came from Brisbane on certain days to spend time with us, and it was great catching up with them. My friend Maree lived in Brisbane, and it was great being close enough to spend time together.

What I've learned about family holidays is how important they are. No matter the length of time or the location of the holiday, it's all about getting together, away from the rollercoaster ride of life, and reconnecting with each other as a family unit.

28

Friends

I have the most amazing friends. I still have a small handful of close female friends that I've known for over twenty years, and I haven't really made any new ones. Finding and keeping a handful of true close friends who like me warts and all is such a special thing. Most of us have lots of acquaintances, and I've met many people on committees or at the school over the years that I consider friends, but I would not include them in that special inner circle.

Cate, a friend from my inner circle, came to visit for the weekend one June. It was during the local winter races and I worked the bar for my son's school camp, which I must say was the most fun I'd had all year. Yes, I hear you. I need to get a life. No argument there. But with four kids, my life is in a different phase.

It had been over two years since I'd been to the races, and the previous time had also been when a friend came to visit. James had taken the kids to Charters

Towers to visit his mum and dad, so the house was a bachelorette pad. OMG, how nice was that.

I went to a nearby town on the Friday to get my hair done, and drove home in time to pick up Cate from the airport. We went straight to a bottle shop, and bought four bottles of wine and a four-pack of Bacardi Breezers. Then we picked up some funny movies, *Pitch Perfect* and *This is 40*, both of which we thought were pretty appropriate considering my impending birthday.

We sat out on the veranda, cracked a bottle of wine and enjoyed the serenity of the house. The only noise to be heard was a pair of happy jack birds cackling—us. Cate phoned in our order for takeaways. Oh, how good was that. No cooking, no demanding children and no husband.

Because we'd had too many wines, Jean took us to pick up our takeaways. When she stopped off at Woolworths we snuck out of the car and caught up with an old ex-work colleague who now packs shelves in the supermarket. He said he was making more money as a packer at Woollies than as a nurse. Seriously? What's going on, Queensland Health? Our friend had so much less responsibility than when he worked as a nurse *and* he got paid more.

Cate and I were very sensible and didn't drink more than two bottles of wine. We were pacing ourselves and trying to improve our 'piss fitness', according to Cate.

The next morning was race day, so we had a relaxed morning. We went to the local coffee shop, and then bought some nibblies to take to the races with us. I was still in a state of disbelief that we had the house to ourselves. Not only that; it was still clean and the only noise was just the two of us giggling.

Two grown women floating on a natural high, playing music, cracking open a bottle of wine, and getting dressed in our finery for the races.

What a marvellous day we had. We met some other friends and got a table in the shade. We were there for over an hour before the next social butterfly turned up, so we made a dent in the nibblies first and got onto our second bottle of wine. We could buy wine by the bottle, which was a great idea and saved me constantly having to walk up to the bar in my Mount Everest of heels.

I felt great, as I very seldom get the chance to spend time with my close friends, who are all scattered throughout Australia. I'm friendly and have a polite chat to people in town or school, but they don't know me like my friends do. It was a really good feeling to have one of *my* friends to hang out with and not feel like a bit of an outsider in my own hometown for a change.

After lots of laughs and antics, I didn't win too much. The day ended with a bang when we won first and second place, although we didn't come out in front because our method of choosing horses by how cool their names were wasn't too scientific. One horse's name was Let the Party Begin. That summed us up, but the horse came in somewhere down the track. Another was called Just About Ready, which reminded us of Jean. That one came in at the rear of the field, too, so I'm not good for a race tip anytime soon.

We progressed to dinner at a local restaurant, which was also very nice. Those friends who couldn't make it to the races came to my pre-birthday dinner. I was trying unsuccessfully to make it an unofficial birthday, as I knew I would be away on the actual day, but my godmother's daughter, who I grew up idolising as a kid, made a chocolate birthday cake, which was so sweet of her. My dad always used to make my birthday cake, and it was always chocolate.

I had grand plans of going to the disco after dinner and was hoping I would have some takers to come with me, but everyone else had hit a wall. One couple came along to the disco at the local pub, but not for long, perhaps ten minutes max, so at ten-thirty we went home, with me trying to stifle my disappointment.

I so just wanted to go dancing, even though the music was pretty shit. I'm stuck in the seventies, eighties and nineties music eras. All the modern *dorf-dorf* stuff doesn't do it for me. For those who are into raves it's fine. They can float in some other world and not even realise the crap they call music is being played.

When we got home, Cate went straight to bed. I cracked open a Bacardi Breezer, put on some music, set up my portable DVD player, played *Pitch Perfect* again, and folded clothes. Yes, I hid in my laundry folding clothes. Is this what life has become? I thought. I don't get to dance at the disco so I put on my own playlist and do my own thing?

I texted a more mature friend of mine and told her what I was doing. She sent back: *Ha, you sound like Mrs Brown at the hen party.* Mrs Brown had been the only one wanting to party. OMG, I thought, is this who I am? There I was, nearly forty, a mother of four, and having my own dance-off in the laundry. Talk about multitasking.

June was a social month. Constance, one of my dearest friends, also came to visit. She had wanted to surprise me, but her mum had phoned three days before and while chatting away asked me to send the quilts back with Constance. I told her it was fine, but that I didn't know when that might be. When I said that, the penny dropped for Constance's mum as she belatedly realised it was supposed to be a surprise.

But I love surprises, and that was a fabulous one. I was so happy at the news that Constance was coming it took all my strength not to burst into tears.

She arrived the Saturday of the annual show and we had a lovely time catching up. James propped up the bar and didn't get home until nearly ten pm, knowing it was supposed to be my night out with Constance. On cue, he made a big deal about it, and to shut him up, Jean, resplendent in her red dressing gown, took Constance and me back to the showgrounds, where we sat in the car for nearly two hours people watching. When we were sure James would be asleep, we headed home again.

Again, I so wanted to go out and dance the night away in the bull dust. The fireworks were amazing, and they're always followed by a live band. But Constance had driven six hours that day to get there, was tired and didn't feel like socialising.

I waited for her to go to sleep, as I didn't want her to feel bad about me going out without her, and sent a text to Jean asking her to come back and get me. I told her I'd meet her on the dirt road, as I didn't want the lights from her car shining in on Constance and waking her. I snuck out the back door and, footloose and fancy free, went back to the music.

I only got two dances before the band stopped playing, but it was still fun socialising and talking to other people. That's something I miss sometimes—just going out with friends, dancing and laughing. I can count on one hand the number of times I've done that in the past ten years. And it's always the times out that you haven't planned for that end up being the best fun.

At two-thirty am I got a lift home with Alanah and another friend, Kezia. Kezia was so good: she turned off her lights as we got close to our gate, and instead of driving in did a 360-degree turn on the dirt road.

It was so funny at the time. Here I was, a wife and mother of four, sneaking in and out of the house like a naughty teenager about to be caught by her parents. I didn't even do that as a teenager. My father would always say, 'I trust you, Tara. Don't ever break my trust.' That was enough to make me make smarter choices, as I adored him and didn't want to upset him.

I never told Constance that I had snuck out like a naughty schoolgirl to go dancing.

One August I went to the annual gift fair in Melbourne to look for stock to re-energise my shop. I was lucky enough to have two nights and three days away by myself. I needed the trip on so many levels, most importantly to have time out from the rollercoaster that is my life. My little shop has been a refuge and an enemy all rolled into one. James hates it, as he feels it takes time away from him. OMG. Men.

Anyone who has come with me to a gift fair knows that I don't stop all day. I have a big breakfast in the morning before I get there and I just walk all day. I'm focused and am there for one reason only: to look for different and unusual gifts. If someone is with me and wants something to eat or drink they have to say so or die of thirst and hunger.

No one came with me this time, and I walked and walked all day, looking at stalls. At the end of the day I met up with my friend Karen and her mum, who were in Melbourne also. We went over to the casino and had dinner, and of course with dinner had a bottle of very nice red wine. Then we decided to have another bottle of this glorious red wine. Karen's mum only had one glass, so Karen and I split the remaining wine.

At eight pm we all headed into the casino and Karen showed me how to play blackjack, which was fun. I only had twenty dollars, so thankfully I had a few wins, which made my money last longer. In the meantime we were still drinking house red, not as nice as the earlier stuff but at this stage it would do. I hadn't had anything to eat since breakfast, apart from our recent dinner, and the wine went straight to my head.

Karen and I thought we were just *so* much fun and everyone else in that part of the casino was *so* serious and boring. They were all taking the whole gambling thing very seriously and we were the only ones cracking a smile. We even told one guy behind that blackjack table, whom we nicknamed Virgil, that we were probably the most fun he had had all night. Not only were we drunk, but delusional as well.

Karen's mum thought it was time for us to leave, as we had a big day ahead of us. We protested and told her she was no fun. In the end we relented and left. If we hadn't, they might have thought to kick us out anyway as security was circling us like a school of great white sharks.

We were near the toilets and laughing about something when it happened. All I can say is thank god it was winter and I had leggings on. Yep, I started to pee my pants. It was trickling down my legs. When the other two women asked what was wrong, I confessed. Well, they just about combusted with laughter.

Thank goodness there were some baby wipes in my handbag. I went into the toilet, removed the leggings, cleaned my legs and shoes, and marched out again pretending nothing was wrong. Karen's mum nicknamed me PP, and we laughed over that unplanned moment for hours.

The taxi dropped me off at my hotel first. I have no memory of getting out of the taxi and walking into the hotel, or getting to my room. I have vague memories of climbing into the spa and washing out my leggings. Apparently I phoned another friend, and I phoned James, who was not impressed with my ramblings, to say the least. He goes to bed about eight pm and it would have been ten pm when I called him. It was obvious that I was very drunk. I was in trouble. James was not too thrilled in the first place about me being out and having a good time while he was at home minding the kids.

I sometimes feel sure it would give James great satisfaction if I were miserable every time I go away. Never let onto your husband that you're enjoying yourself too much. God forbid. That would be a sin.

What I've learned about friendship is that having a handful of amazingly fabulous friends is worth way more than knowing dozens of acquaintances. I'm a very lucky person to have the friends I do.

29

Appearances

People can be funny. When Jean had to have surgery at the Wesley Hospital in Brisbane, I went with her for support. I stayed at the units across the road from the hospital and had to walk up a hill to visit her every day for three days, sometimes two or three times a day.

Well, it was one hell of a hill. It was so steep I could have used it as a ski slope.

Apparently the hill is known as Killer Hill, or Heart Attack Hill, and I understood why after my first walk up it. OMG. I was so puffed and my breathing was so laboured that if I hadn't still had my fibroid uterus, I would have looked like I was in labour. My chest was tight and I thought, here we go, Heart Attack Hill is claiming its first customer for the day.

On my way back down, I passed an elderly lady carrying shopping bags and climbing towards the top. She wasn't even puffing, which made me ashamed of

I'M FORTY

how unfit I was. I couldn't believe it. I've been riding my exercise bike between twenty to thirty kilometres most evenings while watching TV and obviously even that wasn't enough to prepare me for Killer Hill.

I noticed how controlled most people were in trying to walk up the hill. No one was as obviously out of breath as me, panting away. No, they were all very composed and concentrating on their measured breathing, but I could see that they were just as puffed as me.

What I've learned about appearances is how concerned people are about keeping up the act of all is well. Huff and puff and gasp for air if you have to. There is no shame in being human.

30

Exercise

I wish someone had told me in my twenties how hard it would be to get my figure back when I entered the new thirties. OMG. It's so hard. My last child finally ended it for me. Before Thomas was born, I could still fit into my size ten–twelve clothing, but now I'm a size fourteen, with a mummy-belly.

I know, I know. People tell me that I should be proud of it. After all, I have four beautiful children to show for it. What a bunch of hogwash, I say. Be gone, mummy-tummy.

And then there's my boob size, which, pre-children, was a pert size C. Many a time my girlfriends told me that my boobs were amazing and suggested I should go in a wet T-shirt competition. Did I appreciate what I had in my twenties? Oh no. I took my great, pert boobs for granted and in my deluded state thought I would always have them.

When my first baby arrived, my boobs exploded into a walking milk bar, with the prime purpose of feeding the baby. With the second and third child, they shrivelled up into dehydrated prunes. Then came the fourth, and a massive explosion in size, obviously so the dairy bar could return. Since then they haven't shrunk back down; they've remained super-sized. It's like I'm walking around with two watermelons on my chest, but not pert watermelons. Oh no, they're drooping watermelons.

Twenty years ago I was too conservative to appreciate what I had, and missed the chance to show them off a bit more. Now I wish I could show them off less; they're so in your face it's ridiculous.

I want to go into my new thirties at least one dress size down, which would be a size twelve. Downsizing my size-F boobs and my caesarean-created tummy dewlap has posed a more difficult task than I anticipated, but it *will* happen.

Having a hysterectomy has put a halt to the whole sit-up thing, but I have a few weeks to go before my birthday to turn this mummy-tummy into a yummy-tummy. As for the boobs, I think they're here to stay.

Today I'm wearing a black dress with a V-neck collar and it's not even winter yet. I have a scarf draped strategically around my neck, in forty-degree heat, to hide my droopy watermelons. But as I wear a good-quality underwire bra, they don't appear to the average person as droopy watermelons. Instead, they're just about sitting under my chin, being lifted by the underwire.

When I do lose the centimetres around my waistline I doubt that I'll decrease in boob size, so I'll still be a size fourteen above the waist. It's very difficult getting things to fit nicely, where the buttons on my tops aren't gaping and showing off my bra.

My nurse's uniform dress gapes at bra level, but I refuse to increase my dress size to sixteen. Instead I give the patients and staff a bit of a peepshow, with subtle glimpses of my bra between buttons. If they're that desperate that they have to check out my protruding bra, then go hard. Which, I might add, one female nurse did.

This particular nurse told me at the end of the shift that she had been checking out my bra all day. She also has big boobs and wanted to know the make of my bra. So off we went into the vacant high-dependency room and I revealed all, to my waistline, so she could see the label on the back of the bra.

I own a cross-trainer and I was given an exercise bike, but I haven't utilised them of late, at least not as much as I used to. I prefer the exercise bike, not because I think it works better for me but because I hate standing for any length of time. At least when I'm using the bike I can sit down and still exercise.

My plan was to use the bike while I'm watching my TV shows during the week, so I dragged the bike into the lounge room. It worked well for a while and then I had to go away for a week. Getting back into routine was hard, but I do have willpower on my side and I've promised myself I'll get into it again.

I came up with another idea to get back some semblance of a figure and control the mummy-tummy, and that was dancing. I thought about my pre-children era. Every weekend I used to go out dancing until the wee hours of the morning. I'm sure it helped with my fitness level. So I made up an exercise playlist on my iPhone, songs that will get me boogieing for at least half an hour. The music takes me back to my dancing-queen days. It's really quite escapist.

One afternoon I was down in the bedroom, lost in the moment, singing and dancing away to the music, and forgot all about finishing cooking dinner. Thomas, the youngest, was in the room with me and he kept getting cranky as he didn't like my choice of music. I told him that was too bad, as it was me-time.

Then Henry came in, followed by Ann, and caught me in the act. They both just about combusted with giggles at their mum's dancing style. They thought they were so clever. Ann told me I looked good and that it was great to see how people danced in the old days. Then she asked me to do more old-time dancing so they could videotape it.

Between the three kids, they burst my bubble. My moment of pretending I was out on the razzle-dazzle while actually in the confines of my bedroom came to a screeching halt, the moment lost.

When their father came home, the big mouths couldn't wait to tell him all about it. Ann couldn't wait to spill the beans and then wanted me to show James how I dance. I just shook my head and walked away. I told them that before they came along their father and I actually had a life and he had seen me dance many times before.

What I've learned is to do my dancing exercise in the mornings, after the kids have gone to school and before I go to work in the shop. I wish I had listened to the person who told me, when I was in my twenties, that the older you get the harder it is to get back in shape.

31

Facebook and other Social Media

I joined Facebook a couple of years ago to try and arrange a twentieth school reunion. Well, that was a dud. No one appeared very interested. One guy I went to school with totally ignored the messages I sent via Facebook. OMG, was I really that scary at school? Trying to see if anyone else was keen to catch up was like herding sheep.

It appears the people I went to school with are no longer interested in seeing who married who, how many kids we all have, what jobs we do, and whether the popular girls in class have kept their looks or we wall flowers came up the ranks and passed them by.

Maybe that's it. Maybe they're too scared to front up. The hot ones may not be the best-looking girls at school anymore, with every guy hanging off their every word. And those cute guys we used to try and get to look at us have probably let themselves go.

Either way, the planned reunion idea fizzled out. I still kept my Facebook page, but our green parrot is no longer my profile picture. I've stepped up and finally posted a recent picture of myself. Maybe that was the problem. Everyone thought a parrot was trying to organise the reunion.

I was advised that when someone requests to be my friend, I should just go ahead and confirm them, as the more the merrier. In the last month I confirmed three people as friends, who I promptly had to delete and block.

There are some seriously weird people out there. All were guys. One guy was becoming quite suggestive, and when I looked at his page I thought he might have been eyeing me off to join his harem. Oh my Lord, where do they come from? This guy started calling me 'gorgeous' and wanted to meet for coffee. I don't think so. Did he not read my status, which states that I'm married and live in a remote outback town? Where on earth did he think he was coming from? Seriously. From now on I definitely will not be confirming any old person as a friend on Facebook.

I can see how young people or lonely people get caught with this sort of thing. I got my Gen Y sister to remove Harem Guy, and asked my Gen Y shop assistant/friend to remove Mr Meet Me for Coffee. I was actually a bit nervous. Do they know where I live? I'm a mother of four, the figure isn't what it used to be (I'm working on this), and it's not long before I turn twenty-one again.

As to the 'like' thing on Facebook, how on earth does one get people to 'like' your Facebook page?

There's stuff that comes through my personal page with thousands of 'likes.' It's absolute crap. I can't even get to a hundred and fifty 'likes' on my shop page so I can give away a hamper. I don't always have the time to check my page, but now that my gift shop is on Facebook I thought I should be more vigilant. I started running a competition where the winner would get a hamper worth $150. I thought it would so easy, judging by the quality of other things people 'liked', but I still haven't given that hamper away.

Unless I have a belly full of wine, or Southern Comfort, I'm quite conservative by nature. That's when the outgoing Gemini personality kicks in, the miss-personality, life-and-soul-of-the-party Gemini. Other Geminis will get what I mean.

What it is with people writing their every thought all over Facebook? Seriously. Go see a counsellor. And the language is appalling. One day I read one that said they were going to mow their lawn. Really? That's great, but who cares? If someone wants to break in, they can go in the front door, because they know you won't hear them while you're out the back mowing.

I notice some people use Facebook as a tool to vent, but do we all need to know about the 'slutty whore' they thought was going home with them but decided not to? Do we need to know they're going to fight her the next time they see her down the pub, but still maintain that they aren't gay? Hello. They've just put it all over Facebook that they were getting it on with some chick and they're the same sex.

I am *so* glad Facebook didn't exist when I was going out, and there were no iPhones for people to take

I'M FORTY

photographic evidence of our wonderful behaviour and put it all over Facebook or, god forbid, YouTube.

A good friend and I often giggle about the time she decided to do a strip on the roof of her cousin's mother in-law's house and they were trying to get her down before she fell. These days, that would have made YouTube for sure. But it didn't exist then so our crazy antics are for our memory banks only, or when our wonderful mates remind us of choking down at the front of the Gregory Hotel. With no photographic evidence, we can feign innocence and declare, 'It wasn't me. They must have mistaken me for someone else.'

Another friend of ours did 'the wild thing' on the footpath in front of the Main Roads Office, in the main street one dark night. God help us; that would definitely have made social media.

At the Melbourne Cup carnival last year, the first day was Derby Day. I had my trip all planned and had bought tickets to see the musical *South Pacific*, at a cost of nearly two hundred dollars. After a long day at the races, Constance and I got the bus driver to drop us off at the theatre, as we were running late after getting separated from the rest of the group. Jean and my sister Louise were already inside so we had to wait for the first set to finish before being shown to our seats.

Through the first half of the production I started to get a headache. After the break I took some Merysndol, and then had a drink of free wine. Consequently I kept nodding off through the second act and apparently snoring (although I'm yet to be convinced of that). I was very annoyed at myself.

The show finished and we headed for the exit, but it was not to be. Constance was behind me and I told her I felt like vomiting. That was strange for me because I don't vomit if I can help it.

We got out onto the footpath and I told Constance I felt faint, and walked over to where I thought I saw a seat. I walked straight into a glass window, bumped my head and went down on the ground, landing in a smelly ashtray. When I was coming around and trying hard to open my eyes, I could hear Constance, who was a nurse, taking control. Someone put a wet cloth over my face.

The manager of the theatre was very unimpressed by such a commotion. How dare someone faint on her footpath at the front of her theatre? We got no help or compassion from her. She just kept telling the other three to get me off the footpath. I could hear Constance saying she would if she could get a taxi. Someone made the comment that I might have been on drugs. OMG, really? Constance stated that I definitely wasn't, but didn't let on that I had taken some Merysndol for a headache.

Jean kept going on about that fact that I had fainted and landed in an ashtray with my legs open, which I suppose was important but who cares. Louise was panicking. On the way home in the taxi she kept asking who wears white underpants under a black dress. It entered my mind that at least no one had videotaped me with their iPhone and how mortified I would be if it ended up on YouTube.

This is what social media has done to us. Never mind that I felt like crap and had made a spectacle of myself. All that worried me was that someone might have filmed it. OMG, the shame of that.

So that was my after-Derby-Day experience. I had tried to be cultured and go to the theatre, and I had *so* been looking forward to seeing *South Pacific*.

What I've learned about social media is that if you happen to embarrass yourself, make sure it's somewhere where there's no phone reception.

32

Parties

Something happens to a woman when they become a mother. They lose their identity to the extent that they don't know how to socialise with adults in a social setting anymore.

Nothing changed for James when we had kids; he still went out when he wanted to, getting home in the wee hours of the morning and thinking for some reason that I might feel like some affection, which he now knows is not a happening thing. There's more chance of snow in our outback town before he gets any.

I had an older woman tell me once that when making the bed, I should tuck my husband's side of the top sheet in tightly. I then get under the top sheet, and when my husband gets into bed there will be one layer of sheet between us. He will think he's being romantic or sexy, but it's more like a pair of hands groping their way out of a grave in the dark. She told me that by the time he's fumbled around trying to get to me he will be sick of the whole idea, roll over and fall into a deep snoring fit, resembling a grizzly bear going into hibernation.

I must admit I've never had to try this sheet trick; a quick firm *no* has always sufficed. But I have been guilty of crushing up a Phenergan tablet and putting it in a cup of tea that I lovingly offered to make James, just so he would shut up and go to sleep. At three am I don't care to hear who was talking to whom, or who was dancing with whom at the disco, especially when I have to get up in three hours to attend to four kids while he sleeps on.

I'm a bit over going to parties these days and being the unpaid chauffeur. Not once does James ever suggest that he drive so I can have a couple of drinks, or come home with me and the kids when it's time to leave. No, we go to the party and I spend the entire time keeping an eye on the kids, making sure they've eaten.

I have maybe one wine if I'm lucky. James will say he's only having a few beers, but like a small child worried that he's going to be made to go home soon, he starts guzzling them down, checking every so often to see where I am in case I look like I'm making a move to leave.

If one of our children comes grizzling to me saying they're tired, I scan the crowd searching for my husband and where he's hiding hoping it will take me another ten minutes to find him so he can guzzle at least one or two more drinks in that time.

When I track him down I tell him, 'I'm going home now, the kids are tired.'

'Do you need me to come now?' he might ask. 'I'm just having a few drinks with Billy Bob, we haven't done this in ages.'

32 PARTIES

Men have such selective memories. I just sigh and state that I'm leaving.

When the kids were a lot smaller I would make James walk me out to the car and help me put them into their seats. Before I even accelerate the engine to drive home, the kids nearly always fall asleep and then I have to juggle all four of the little darlings from the car to the house and put them to bed. It's *so* annoying. James never comes home with us, so basically this scenario happens every time.

So I've lost all interest in going to parties with the kids in tow. When they're older and I don't have to carry them out of the car, things might change.

I used to be the life of the party if I was in the mood for it, but something changes the minute you fall pregnant. Hanging out with a bunch of drunks soon lost its appeal when all I could have was a wine spritzer. Until then I'd never realised how much crap flows from people's mouths after a few alcoholic beverages.

I went to a twenty-first party recently. A friend babysat for me and drove us to the party so I could have a couple of drinks. Before I even left home I had to have one drink just to get into social mode. I used to see Fay, Jean's mum, do that, and now it's happening to me.

I spent the entire night with a couple of women talking about life in general. We sat down to eat dinner and that was it. Basically I didn't move again. A fellow guest and I chatted and people watched until nearly one am. I tried having a few drinks, but it just wasn't happening for me. I am so out of practice.

Many moons ago I went out with some friends in Townsville and when we were leaving the pub I asked the bouncer to tell us where there was a good place for dancing.

'For your age group—' he began.

'Be *very* careful what comes out of your mouth next,' I said.

Last year we went to a friend's birthday party in a nearby town. I had just had an abdominal-hernia repair the week before, so consequently I was not drinking. James thoroughly enjoyed himself and we had to drive home that night. When it was time to leave he suggested I have a sleep on their lounge.

'No,' I said. 'Nearly everyone's gone, it's one am and we need to get going.'

Well, all the way home he carried on like a pork chop. Every ten minutes he pulled over to pee. He was worse than a man with a prostrate problem or a woman with a urinary tract infection. Every time he got out of the car, he kept trying to coax me out of the driver's side so he could drive. Not likely. Instead of an hour and a half, it took us nearly three hours to get home.

At the latest party we went to, I asked if he had had something to eat as I could see he was drinking rum. The other men standing with him had just finished eating, so you can understand their laughter when I asked the question. He said he'd had a steak sandwich with onion. The other husbands just burst into laughter, because the food on offer was burritos and tacos, the birthday boy's favourite food.

My husband was acting like our ten-year-old son caught out big time in a lie. There wasn't any steak or onion on offer. When I walked away I heard him saying to the other men, 'What sort of party doesn't have steak and onion? Any other party, I would've been right.'

God give me strength. How old was he? Forty. One would think he was one of the twenty year olds there.

An elderly man in his seventies once told me, 'Men don't grow up until they're forty.'

At the time, James was thirty-seven. 'My husband might not make forty,' I said. 'I'll have disposed of him before then.'

He did make it to forty and there are some, albeit small, signs of maturity when it comes to drinking; however, time will tell.

I feel very strongly that when we have the responsibility of kids, only one parent at a time can drink. I couldn't bear the embarrassment if one of the kids got sick and I had to take them up to the hospital in a taxi, pretend I hadn't been drinking, and fabricate a story about not noticing the car had a flat and it was too dark to change it. I'm a nurse and I've seen all sorts of situations like that, and no one is getting any ammunition against me on my watch.

It's even difficult to try and get away for a break, unless it falls on a weekend. Every time I organise someone to mind the kids so I can go away, it always ends up with some sort of drama. The last time James and I went away together, on our own, it was only the second time since we had had a family.

OMG. Once, when we were at an eighteenth birthday party for James's goddaughter, Jean told me my number-26 personality was coming out.

'Tara is a Gemini and has about twenty-five personalities,' she said. 'I've known her for thirty-five years and I've never seen this personality before.'

Everyone at the party was a close friend of the family. I had made a hotpot of slow-cooked ribs and for some reason I'd been on edge and cranky most of the day. Off we trotted with four kids and a husband in tow. James was sad and sorry for himself as he had been out the night before. Mind you, it was me who had suggested he go out the night before so he would be too sick to drink again at this party. I was concerned that if there was someone there who annoyed him, it would be him getting in a blue and not me.

So I blame James. I just wanted to take four Bacardi Breezers along to the party and that would have suited me, but he suggested I take a bottle of Southern Comfort and a bottle of ginger ale. Consequently, I was sitting there socialising, drinking my Southern with a dash of ginger ale, and cackling away like a witch, much to his embarrassment. James said he was going and he left the kids behind, so his cousin had to drop our kids home with his cousins' kids, as they were sleeping over.

Well, apparently after being introduced to my sister's cute Scottish boyfriend, I was Miss Social Butterfly, working my charms, especially after being told how hot I looked and that I didn't look a day over forty. Hmm, I decided I liked this guy, and then I proceeded to vomit all over myself.

Alanah and Jean dragged me up to the bathroom to clean me up. I followed that by hanging off the clothesline for support, as my legs no longer served any purpose to my body. *Saturday Night Fever* then took hold of me and I wanted to go dancing. I'd heard there was a great band playing, but much to my annoyance it had closed and the only pub left to go party at was the hotel.

OMG. Jean and Kezia waited outside and Alanah went in with me. I took one look around and thought, no, I'm not staying in here. One quick scan in my drunken, delirious state and I could tell this pub was full of unsavoury characters. I promptly announced that decision to Alanah top note. By that stage she was hoping the ground would swallow her up whole.

They tried to put me in the night-patrol car to take me home. Not on your life, petal. I wasn't getting in that car. I ran away from them and headed back to the original party.

I flagged down friends who were driving by and had been working the bar. It took twenty minutes for them to persuade me to get in the car while I proceeded to educate them, in my drunken delirium, about my views on husbands and life. Profound stuff. I can tell you, words of wisdom poured out of my mouth. Thank god they found it amusing.

At one point I started yelling, 'Man down.'

My crazy youngest sister came running from nowhere, eyes popping out like dogs' balls, thinking I was in trouble. At least, even in her crazed state, she was coming in as backup.

There was nothing wrong with me, although a good slap across the face wouldn't have gone astray. What possessed me at that stage was anyone's guess. After Louise saw I was just being as crazy as her, she took her Scottish boyfriend home.

After we left the hotel I flailed my arms around like a broken fan, showing them how I would have fought the unsavoury characters in the pub, if they had heard me. I kept poking and pushing Jean in the arm all night, insisting she 'catch up'. There wasn't a hope in hell she could have caught up with me, thank the

Lord. One drunken (usually sensible, mature) female beyond the point of return was all anyone could have coped with that night.

That was when Jean told Kezia that she had known me for thirty-five years and had never seen this personality before. 'I've heard of her,' she said, 'but I never thought I'd meet her in this lifetime.'

The first moral to this story is not to take a twenty-six-ounce bottle of Southern Comfort to a party and think you won't drink it. I hadn't been that drunk in ten years and to still have blanks about the night in question, even as I type these words ... *so* naughty.

Thank god I was surrounded by non-judgemental people who didn't hold my moments of psychotic madness against me. Instead they just about peed their pants laughing about it, as I'm usually so controlled and together. I suppose there comes a point when even the most controlled of us have a few stitches that will come undone if we're stretched too far.

The second moral is not to go drinking after being uptight and on edge all day; when you feel like you're only being held together by a piece of string. And that's when you're sober. Imagine what you will look like drunk.

Miss Twenty-Sixth Personality is now going to be put to rest, never to resurface again.

What I've learned about parties is not to let your piss fitness deteriorate or you'll end up embarrassing yourself. And also, it shouldn't be years between fun nights out.

33

Doctors' Appointments

I usually arrive late at the doctor's surgery, with one too many kids in tow, carrying toys that aren't needed, and trying to make do with wiping four kids' runny noses with my last remaining tissue.

One of my pet hates is to have to take all the kids to the doctor at once. I prep them before they go in there, threatening them with near death if they start fighting. The usual scenario is that they start arguing over a toy. One will start whining and it's all on.

Our doctor is just fabulous with them. He takes one look and calls our surname. He has Ann convinced she's going to be a doctor; she was fascinated by all the injections I had to have during each pregnancy.

I even had to take Thomas with me while I had a pap smear. Thankfully he was too young to know what was going on, but he lay up next to me on the bed like he was the one being examined. Once I even had to take him with me when I went for an abdominal cat scan. The technician was *so* nice and gave him some colouring-in to do while he watched Mum through the glass shield. When it was all over I had to tackle the hour and a half's drive home, so luckily I didn't react to the dye.

It's very hard to get an appointment to see our doctor. The doctors at our clinic are so respected and in demand that patients drive for three hours to see them. On more than one occasion I've had an appointment for one child, but by the time that appointment date arrives I'll usually have another one sick, so it's a rare treat for our doctor if I only turn up with one child for him to see.

Doctor's receptionists can be like prison guards. I'm not sure if that's part of the job description, or part of their key selection criteria, as it's so hard sometimes to get to see the doctor. They aren't all bad, but phew, there are some that make me feel I'm back at school and am getting a dressing-down from the principal.

What I've learned from doctor's appointments is to try not to let anyone in the family get sick. It's such a pain in the butt when one of them gets sick and I have to drag everyone to the doctor.

34

Women's Health

Well, today is my birthday and it's a pretty significant number, so they tell me. And where am I spending it? At the Wesley Breast Clinic having my breasts crunched, probed and poked. Other women have told me that it hurts when you have a mammogram; however, the whole squashing them thing doesn't really bother me too much. Maybe it's because after breastfeeding four children, all the sucking, gnawing and chewing has meant all sensation in my nipples has been deadened.

Breasts always remind me of little puppies—or, in my case, big puppies—in the way kids would stretch them out to try and make the milk flower faster. Their little hands were constantly pushing at the other breast, so it's no wonder that having a mammogram doesn't hurt. Four kids succeeded in breaking in my breasts to mammograms years ago.

I've been having ultrasounds since I was twenty-four, as I have a family history of breast cancer. I was recently informed that because I had an uncle with breast cancer, I have to start having MRI scans. Great. Another check-up. Thank god I don't suffer from claustrophobia.

Thankfully I didn't have to have a needle biopsy like the last two times I had issues. As the lump was under my nipple, they had to do a fine-needle aspiration. James asked me if it hurt, and the only way I could describe it to him was to suggest that he got a fine needle, inserted it into one of his testicles, withdrew some liquid, and then took a couple of Panadol after it.

Pap smears are another embarrassing and uncomfortable examination that we women have to endure. I'm not sure if every woman can remember her first pap smear, but I sure can. I was about eighteen, and the doctor—who was the only one in town—had known me for many years.

'It'll feel cold and hard,' he told me, 'because it's metal. Unlike a penis, if you clench down on this it'll hurt. So try and relax.'

Relax. Why do they always say that when you have a pap smear, especially the male doctors? They've never had a large metal object wedged between their legs.

A few weeks after this experience, I commenced working at the local hospital and had to see that same doctor every day. Thank goodness my mother had brought me up with the mentality that they're doctors and have seen it all before.

What I've learned about health is that there's really nothing we women can do except get on with it and pray for a speedy examination.

35

Television

Thank the Lord for TV shows, especially the evening ones. I need the pure escapism to help me block off reality and transport me to another place and time.

I love most genres. I watched *Grey's Anatomy* from the very first episode and pretty much planned my week around it. If James came home and said he had a work dinner on the night *Grey's* was showing, everything hinged on whether I could attend it with him and still make it home in time to see my show.

I didn't want anyone speaking to me, or phoning me, when it was on. James even knew that he could forget about watching football if *Grey's* was on that night. During one episode, he and the kids tried being stupid and serenading me with a guitar while I was watching it. I came so close to grabbing that guitar and either smashing it or shoving it somewhere nasty.

A few years ago when I was at a spa retreat with my very good friends Maree and Constance, we made sure we didn't go to dinner the night *Grey's* was on. Both Constance and I wanted to watch it, but Maree was horrified at the very thought. We're all nurses. Maree thinks the show is rubbish, but she's only looking at the medical aspect of the show, whereas Constance and I concentrate more on the stories of the individual characters.

We snuggled up in our beds, enjoying the show, while Maree made annoying comments from the sidelines. We had to tell her to go to sleep; she was ruining the experience for us. It was my first break away from the kids in such a long time, without having a baby permanently attached to me. We had left James in Brisbane with the four kids, and he was weaning Thomas, who had to go cold turkey from the milk bar.

Fay, Jean's mum, was just the same about *Grey's*. It was our favourite show. She died in October 2011, so I sit there and pretend she's still sharing it. Jean quite often says, 'It's not real. These people are not real, Tara.'

I know that, but that's the beauty of film and TV. I can lose myself in the story for those brief moments and forget there's a mountain of folding and filing to do.

I used to love the antics of *Brothers and Sisters*. My cousin Leith and I watched it together, despite the fact that we live twenty hours from each other. During the ad breaks we would make comments to and fro by text message.

However, if they kill off an actor I love, I axe that show and don't bother watching it again. I was devastated when the Matthew character died in *Downton Abbey*, so I might not watch season three. Thank goodness I have some time to think about it before making a decision. Leith and I loved the Matthew-and-Mary love story, and

Maggie Smith as the grandmother. We both love how the grandmother gets every problem solved, however devious her methods.

I've been staying up very late on a Tuesday night to watch a cop show called *Against the Wall*. Last night was the season finale and it left me wondering which guy she was going to choose. It appears we'll never know. It was like Scarlet O'Hara all over again. Will she or won't she get Rhett back? I've never read the sequel to *Gone with the Wind*. I just can't bring myself to do it.

I went online to see if I could cheat and find out who the character in *Against the Wall* would choose, only to discover they aren't making a season two. Who decides that? And why would Channel 7 purchase the rights to a show knowing we're not going to see the end of the series sequel? There's so much rubbish on, and yet a good show like that got axed. It was on at midnight, but I always made sure I stayed up to watch it, so I'm feeling very cheated at the moment.

Mind you, during my year of travelling overseas I missed out on TV altogether and actually found it quite liberating. Perhaps it was due to the fact that I was living a very interesting, adventure-packed moment in time that deserved my full attention.

What I've learned from TV is to try not to get too involved in a show's characters. As Jean keeps reminding me, they're just an escape from reality.

36

Reading

Reading is almost non-existent for me these days. I love reading, and before children used to read a lot, but now I'm confined to flicking through magazines. I can count on two hands how many books I've read over the last ten years.

My problem is that if I read a book and it happens to be a good one, I will read, read and read. I've been known to read right through the night. But the kids still need to be fed. So begrudgingly I will get up and give them breakfast, but all I really want to do is keep reading. So I tend to wait until the Christmas holidays and read a book or two then.

Reading takes me to another world, another life, and if it's a great book the details and description in a book far outweigh any film made from that book.

I remember reading *The Bridges of Madison County*. I loved that book and shed tears over it, but when the movie was made, although they had an amazingly talented cast, the actors were not who I had envisioned to play the parts.

My prize possession is an original-cover edition of *Gone with the Wind*. Although the movie left out some things, it's still an all-time favourite of mine.

James has read all the *Game of Thrones* books and is amazed at how faithfully the episodes have kept to the books' storyline, but it's *so* frustrating watching them with him because I get a running commentary every time someone on the screen speaks.

Fifty Shades of Grey is going to be an interesting movie, because if it stays true to the book it could be considered soft porn. The things that man does to her. OMG. The book is so hot and raunchy, and I honestly don't know which actors and actresses would be prepared to go to those extremes for the role. If they're going to make the movie, it has to capture the book at its fullest or it will be a flop.

What I've learned about reading is that it sometimes doesn't pay for me to watch a movie after I've read the book, especially if they've made changes.

And I've also learned that I should pick up a book and start reading again, but restrict it to during the holidays. That way it doesn't matter if I look like a walking zombie after pulling an all-nighter reading a great story.

Small Towns

Living in a small community can be great, as everyone knows everyone, and I can go to the supermarket and talk to someone I know in just about every aisle.

Growing up as a kid in such a small, isolated town could be very annoying, however. What sometimes started out as a quick trip to do the grocery shopping could result in being away from home for hours; my father stopped to chat to every single person who crossed his path. I always had to make sure I told him everything I did, good, bad or indifferent, as I could guarantee that someone would always tell him my business and embroider the story.

The downside to living in a small community is the cliques, and there are quite a lot of little groups like that here in my town. Some people are quite nice and some are anything but nice. I just look at the not-so-nice ones and think that one day they'll be coming up to the hospital feeling sick and vulnerable, needing and expecting me to be caring and kind.

That's happened so many times now. I always act the ultimate professional, and I treat them and care for them as well as I can, even if the entire time I'm thinking that a large-bore blunt needle would serve them well. From my many years of nursing, I know that our bodily functions all operate in the same way, whether we're rich, poor or somewhere in between, and karma always catches up with us.

I've noticed, especially over the last few years, that because I don't do coffee mornings or go socialising, some people won't even come into my gift shop. They would rather drive a three-hour return trip to a nearby town, thinking they'll find something nicer when they haven't even taken the time to come in and have a look. It's very frustrating, as I know I stock nice things. I've had people who are not from this town come in and been amazed that such a nice shop exists in a small rural town. They comment on the lovely things and buy stuff they haven't seen before.

What I've learned from living in a small town is to always be myself. People will gossip about me no matter what I do or say.

38

The Arts

I've been on the committee of the Queensland Arts Council since I was eighteen, and I couldn't wait to join. The council used to consist of a group of women led by one man, the president, and when I was a child growing up it was a force to be reckoned with, or so it seemed, as they used to gain a lot of their funds from catering events around town. As a teenager I used to waitress for them.

The main event of the year was the annual art contest, and it was a very prestigious affair. It was the only time of year that my father would don a suit and tie, which was a big deal for him. Each year he would purchase a piece of artwork, but usually not without showing me first. It was our tradition to go down to see the art on display after school, walk around looking at the paintings and then decide together on the artwork he would buy.

So I was introduced to the arts from a very young age and to this day I'm still passionate about bringing the arts to the bush.

When a worldwide exhibition of Renoir's work came to Australia, my friend Lee and I travelled for four days to Sydney so we could see the exhibition, and also *Phantom of the Opera*. Lee had already seen the exhibition in Brisbane, so she didn't really need to see it in Sydney, but we went down to the big smoke anyway, two country girls experiencing the culture of the arts in all its forms.

At eighteen, when I joined the Arts Council, I was just a worker and was happy to be told what to do. That was great, as on the night of the art show I was still able to have a few wines and enjoy the evening without much responsibility. I've shared many a drink at the art show with other members, and even ended up sitting on the footpath outside afterwards. Very classy indeed. One night I had had one too many wines and couldn't even work the tap on the cask wine that I was drinking and had to get someone else to do it for me.

I took on the role of secretary of the Arts Council when I was pregnant with Ann, and have retained that position for eight years. I'm not the world's best secretary, but between the treasurer and me, along with some trusty helpers, we get the job done, and by some stroke of magic things usually turn out fine. I've often joked that if I won Lotto I would pay someone to do the paperwork side of being a secretary. Each year is stressful, but it's getting less intense with time and experience.

Preparing for an art show is very time consuming. We receive entries from all over Queensland, and each entry has to be unpacked, catalogued and displayed. Hopefully as many as possible will be sold, so there will be fewer to package up at the end.

For the last eight years I've always had one, two, or even three kids tagging behind me, being dragged from pillar to post while I set up an art show. All I can do is thank the Lord for portable DVD players. They have been a godsend for my sanity and those around me. Last year I spent the entire time bribing my youngest with chocolate-coated donuts if he behaved. I'm aware that's not good mothering, but when setting up for an art show we do what we need to do to survive.

I've even resorted to working there late at night so I don't have to take all the kids with me. As they get older it's getting easier, and next year I won't have any children tagging behind me since they'll all be at school.

Our committee is much smaller now. We definitely don't have the manpower to do much fundraising, so we rely very heavily on sponsorship. We have presented On Tour arts productions, including school-age productions, but, due to politics, the funding for On Tour productions came to an end, and it's now left to individual arts councils to secure productions for their town. After a couple of years of cultural drought, we've had the pleasure of presenting an adults' and children's production, in partnership with Xstrata.

What I've learned from the arts is to do whatever it takes to keep the art show going, and to find ways to support and bring the arts to the bush.

39

Committees

I think everyone should be on a committee, as it's important to give something back to the community. I hope I can instil into my children that it's very important to contribute to the local community, one way or another, and try to lead by example. I support their school functions and am a committee member.

But, OMG, what a nightmare committees can be. Thankfully I'm only on the one committee and it's small, which means fewer personalities to contend with. I made the decision many years ago to stick with only one, and to choose one I feel passionate about.

Whatever the committee, it's best not to have too many women together; otherwise it can turn catty. I've seen firsthand how relatively normal women can turn power mad with the responsibility of being on a committee.

Take the kindergarten committee, for example. I've always avoided being on kindergarten committees.

I've had four children go through kindy and so I'm willing to lend a hand if they need help, but as for being on the committee, that's a different story. I appreciate that someone has to do it, but why do their personalities have to change the minute they join?

What I've learned from committees is how grateful I am for being on a small one, as there are fewer personalities to contend with.

40

My Gift Shop

When I started out there were three other gift shops in town, so now there are four. I was and still am very respectful of the goods that other businesses stock, but I soon discovered the same respect was not going to be shown to me. I'm not sure if it's the same everywhere, but retail in a small country town can be a very bitchy, competitive business.

I always try to stock brands and items that the other retailers don't stock. For instance, when I first started out no one else in town sold scented candles, no one sold gourmet food, and no one else did gift hampers. Now quite a few other shops offer the same. That's been quite soul destroying and discouraging, as I all I wanted to do was bring quality, affordable and different gifts to the town I have called home for my entire life.

I try to maintain a positive attitude, regardless of the actions of others around me, but I've noticed lately that I'm becoming quite jaded. Unfortunately, this town has little groups that ally with one shop or another, and because I'm so busy with kids and family, friends, nursing and trying to run my shop, I don't have the time, or, to be honest, the inclination to be part of any backstabbing small-town group.

But that is life, and it's the stronger person who can rise above that. I used to be close friends with someone I met through nursing. Well, I thought we were close friends, but over time I realised that we were only friends because I served a purpose for her. When she didn't need me to do things for her — babysit her kids and so on — the friendship fizzled out, mainly because I became hurt and shut down.

That's one of my major flaws. I tend to give and give and give until it hurts. I think and care about people, and try to be there for my friends and family as much as I can, even when they aren't being very nice in return. It eventually catches up with me, even if it takes years until the penny finally drops and I realise I don't want to be a doormat any longer.

As I've matured, I find it doesn't happen so often anymore. That must be another benefit to entering the new thirties, that through time and life experiences we finally work people out a lot quicker.

I've always been a relatively good judge of character, but I've been known to bury my head in the sand on occasion and ignore the truth staring straight at me.

I love having my shop. It's been an amazing experience. I've been taking Ann there since she was two, and the other three kids have tagged along behind me for years too. I had a playpen full of goodies and a portable DVD player there to amuse them, but now that Thomas is at kindy it looks more like a gift shop again.

My shop has been a sanctuary away from housework and everyday chores, and it gives me the opportunity to socialise with people from all walks of life. It allows me to interact with a diversity of people, including customers, retailers and suppliers. I've made some great acquaintances and I don't want to let it go. With lack of support from people and rising electricity costs, however, I have to reconsider if it's still worth it, which is nuts, as next year all four children will be in school full time, which will be the perfect opportunity for me to give my shop all I can.

I also have a website, but OMG, it's hard to get people to buy online from a webpage. I paid a ridiculous amount of money a couple of years ago for a search-engine-optimisation program. The plan was to get the retailers on the front page of Google, but it cost a small fortune and I reaped no return for my financial outlay.

I think I'm very creative and I do make up wonderful hampers. I can make a great hamper out of anything that has an opening, or space, big enough to hold items. Recently a friend ordered two hampers from me to send to Western Australia. She could have ordered them in Perth and it would have cost her less in postage. When I mentioned that, she said she knew that, but it wouldn't have had the same love and attention to detail that I give my presentations.

It was such a nice feeling to hear her say that, as it's true. Everything I wrap or put together, or buy for the shop from a gift fair, is all about that. I love it, and hopefully someone else will too. Each gift hamper has a lot of thought put into it, and the more information I can get about the person/s who will receive the finished product, the better the hamper is. I never include anything that I wouldn't love to receive myself.

But alas, I'm not very business orientated. I'm not good at selling myself and putting myself out there to show people what a great service I can provide. If I could just be the ideas creator, my life would be complete.

I did accounting at school and really enjoyed it, and at one stage I thought I would like to be an accountant. Before I went backpacking I saved every spare cent for two years and used to be so good at saving money. But now, as I juggle the needs of four kids, husband, mortgage and business, my saving and accountancy skills have fizzled out like a dying sparkler.

Anyone with any business sense would tell me to cut my losses and give up my shop, but something in me keeps going. The people in this town don't realise that I've always felt I've been providing a local service, the same as when I'm nursing and providing a service to the patients, but, much like nursing, it's a thankless role.

I've never charged anymore on my products than the recommended retail price, and it has only been in the last couple of years that I've started adding freight to the product cost. Before that, I stupidly covered that cost myself. See? No business sense. Every other businessperson in their right mind covers their costs.

I've been going to gift fairs for years, so I can personally smell, touch and taste the products I sell. I attend seminars whenever possible and was ahead of my time, in this town, in making sure I kept displays fresh by changing them regularly.

When I started my website I thought that if I could only make my online business a success, I wouldn't have to be so concerned about how many or how few people walk in. I could leave the people of this community behind and hit the bigger market; however, that has not been the case. It's very hard to break into the online shopping community.

What I've learned about owning and running my gift shop is to love what I do, but know when it's time to say enough. However, that's often easier said than done.

41

Giving Presents

It's very important to me that I put a great deal of thought into any gift I give. If I don't like the present I give someone, I don't get any enjoyment out of giving it. I have a birthday book, but I usually remember people's birthdays by their star sign. Sometimes I even buy presents months earlier than needed, especially if I see something that would suit a particular person.

Buying presents for James can be quite difficult. Over the years I've certainly bought him some presents that have been really quite stupid.

I once bought a silly-looking tiger knife for him from Franklin Mint. He mentioned that it looked cool, so I thought he would like it. We hadn't been going out together for long at the time, and when I gave it to him he said he liked it. After about ten years he informed me that it was most likely the stupidest present I had ever bought him.

We've been together nearly twenty years now, and it was only two years ago that I finally nailed the whole present thing for him. I finally saved enough to buy a Waeco fridge-freezer for him, which he can take camping and fishing. James just lives for his next fishing trip.

What I've learned about gifts is that if you wouldn't love to receive the gift yourself, you shouldn't give it.

42

Surgery

OMG. My fortieth is just over the horizon and already I've had to face the daunting process of undergoing a hysterectomy. I never expected to lose my girlie bits while still in my prime, but it was unavoidable.

My hospital stay isn't a pleasant memory. What an experience. Having the privacy of my own room and toilet and bathroom were the only good things about being in that private hospital in Townsville. The nursing care left a lot to be desired. As a nurse myself, I was totally horrified at the attitude of some of the nurses. Some nurses are in the job for all the wrong reasons. By the time I was discharged, I had been made to feel like a drug-seeking hypochondriac. I was given very little support, and almost no compassion for the fact that I had just had major abdominal surgery — through four previous caesarean scars.

As a side effect of the pain relief I was taking, I became extremely constipated. Consequently, and on the day before I was discharged from the hospital I was given a bowel-prep solution to assist with my problem. After a litre and a half of that, I was moving as fast as someone could with a fresh incision wound from hip to hip. My new BF was now a piece of porcelain bowl. I was still getting close to my *new* friend the next morning when my *old* friend came to pick me up.

I spent that night at a friend's place and the next morning I flew home. I was like a walking corpse when I got off the plane. Jean took me to my doctor immediately. I was such a mess. I was in so much pain and very emotional. When I saw the doctor I burst into tears, but between him and another doctor, they soon had my pain under control.

I was admitted to our local hospital for another five days. I have never slept so much in my life. I'm sure it was a combination of finally getting adequate pain relief and the lack of sleep I experienced before going off to have my operation.

I had spent days before the operation preparing myself and preparing the house, as is a mother's lot. Several times I stayed up until three am, and then got up to face the new day at six in the morning. It had been the last week of school, and as always it was full on. With three kids at school, I had to provide plates for three class parties. I cheated, as I also had so much to do at my gift shop before I went for my surgery. I supplied ice creams to William and Henry's classes, and as Ann's class went to the local swimming pool all I had to do was provide her with pocket money to buy a treat at the pool.

I'M FORTY

We left for Townsville on Sunday at seven am. I had been awake from six am on Saturday. I had organised the household, cleaned and cleaned some more, and spent the rest of the day making gift baskets.

This was my usual routine before going anywhere. I always stay up until the early hours of the morning to get everything done. I clean the house and pack the car while James sleeps on. Then I wake him up and he does the driving. This time, however, we had an engagement party to go to on the Saturday evening. The kids and I came home at nine pm, and I told James to be home at midnight. Well, what he agreed to and what he did are two different things.

Midnight came and went. Two am came and went. I was still up. I lay down at three am, only to get a phone call from James at three-thirty am, asking if I could come and pick him up. Well, you can imagine what I said. My answer was a flat denial. I was so annoyed.

Then he asked if I could pick him up as we left town.

'If you're not home soon,' I told him, 'I'll drive to Townsville without you.'

He arrived home at four-thirty and immediately went to sleep. I packed the car, bundled the kids inside and woke him at six-thirty. With me at the wheel, we eventually left town at seven am, after buying greasy food to absorb the grog from the night before.

When we were forty kilometres out of Julia Creek I was starting to get very tired. I had only been driving for one and a half hours, so I hadn't got very far before I was feeling exhausted. I phoned my friend to see if she could talk to me to keep me awake until I got into town, when I could drink V drinks to give me some b-b-bounce and keep me going. Talking to my friend's husband kept me going, and the drinks helped.

James eventually woke up after filling the car with snores and brewery smells, and told me he would be all right to drive when we got to Richmond, which was another two hours away. Yeah, a likely story.

I drove the whole way, and after doing that trip I've decided that fatigue kills more than speed. If you're tired, it really doesn't matter how fast or slow you're driving. Fall asleep and it's all over. However, we made it to Townsville in one piece and dropped the kids off with James's parents at Charters Towers.

That night we stayed with good friends and went to the Cactus Saloon. We had cocktails at happy hour, which were very yummy and the food was great.

On our way home, we all pulled into a new sex shop, Cate and her husband, and James and I. I must admit it was quite tastefully done. The lady behind the counter seemed nice and not at all sleazy. And it didn't have that awful pheromones smell. Some of the objects in that shop were beyond a joke. We came across a butt plug that was nearly the size of a butternut pumpkin.

I was shopping on behalf of a lesbian friend of mine, who was after a U-shaped dildo that both she and her girlfriend could use at the same time. I found one, but it had a knobbly bit on the end so that was no good. She had told me that it couldn't resemble a penis at all.

Cate and I were looking for the silver balls that were used in *Fifty Shades of Grey*, as she is also an avid fan of that trilogy, but they didn't have what we were looking for so we left after having a giggle and a good look around.

I had to fast from midnight for my surgery the next day, so after two more wines I hit the sack, totally exhausted. I was so tired I was sure they wouldn't even have to give me anaesthetic the next morning.

What I've learned from having surgery is that there's a cost to taking that time for myself. There's too much to organize, and the house falls apart when I'm not feeling very well.

43

Travelling with the In-laws

We took James's parents on a trip to Melbourne once, and after that we both vowed never to do it again. His father sat behind me in the car and sighed every two minutes. I kept waiting for him to say 'How long now?'

Every time we bought something to eat, he told us he could buy a burger cheaper at the Burke and Wills Roadhouse back home. When we took them to Lygon Street in Melbourne, we actually had to fib about how much the meal cost. We told him it was only ten dollars.

We went out of our way to show them the Twelve Apostles and Great Ocean Road, which everyone knows has breathtaking scenery, but did he appreciate any of it? No.

When we got out of the car to look at the legendary limestone stacks, the first words he uttered were, 'We drove all this way to see rocks in the ocean.'

All James and I could do was laugh, as this was a man who was planning to travel around Australia when he retired. If his lack of appreciation of the sights we had shown him so far was anything to go by, at that moment it was guaranteed that James's parents would *not* be joining the other grey nomads and going adventuring together.

James's mother is much more adventurous. She embraces a challenge. When the three of us travelled together in Africa, she was at the wheel when we visited a national park. Hawk-eyed James spotted a cheetah and told his mother to keep driving and not stop. He was trying to film it, like David Attenborough, with his mother driving like we were in the Grand Prix, when the cheetah ran in front of us. I had a vision of turning it into road kill and us being permanently deported from Africa. But the cheetah was too quick for the Grand Prix rally driver. Thank the Lord cheetahs are so fast and nimble.

What I've learned from travelling with my in-laws is to take the adventurous one and leave the other one at home.

Chaos and the Big Kids

*P*arenting is such a challenging role. I would put it up there as the hardest job I've ever had to cope with. The last two weeks have been full on, as Henry and Ann have not stopped fighting. As soon as they wake up they start on each other. As soon as they get in the car they start arguing.

When I dropped Ann off at a dance her tennis coach informed me, very matter-of-factly, that she and Henry had been fighting at tennis. OMG. Apparently he threw a tennis ball at her and she exploded and threw a tennis racket back at him.

It's bad enough that they're irritating each other at home, but now it's going public. Getting the homework done is a nightmare. I could choose to be a relaxed mum and not worry about helping them, but that's not being a caring and responsible parent. Explaining to those two little darlings that homework is important, however, pushes me to a point that's its wine o'clock by four pm. Not that I do this, but after doing homework I sure feel like guzzling an entire bottle.

Ann doesn't see the importance of spelling, and Henry doesn't think he needs to extend his sentences past one line. So I play the bad cop and confiscate iPods and Wii. At the moment they're all banned until they improve.

I told my hotheaded daughter how confident and powerful an articulate person could be when they're able to spell and read well. It worked, as she got 14/15 on her next test. Who knew she was such a power freak?

Mind you, the night before that I had had to listen to her claiming she had the worst life in the world, stating that she must be adopted, blah, blah, blah. And then she came out with a real beauty. I was in William's room putting him to sleep when she came in.

'Mum,' she said, 'I just want to tell it to you straight. If I was a monkey you would be ripped to pieces by now.'

OMG. My response to that was to tell her to go to bed. When I told James he just laughed. I still can't believe she said that. Ten minutes later she tried talking to me and I told her she was rude and needed to go to bed. She was shocked at me thinking that what she said was offensive. Funnily enough, her Chinese sign is the year of the monkey.

What I've learned from having older children is to always keep an ample supply of good wine and port on hand so I can drift off to that sandy beach in Hawaii. If all else fails, skull your first glass of wine and pour your second.

45

Personal Space

My aunties and cousins tell me I have to make time for myself. And I do. I hide in the car and quietly contemplate life. There's nothing like the quiet serenity of the car, where I sit and regain my strength. Or I watch something on my laptop when chaos is erupting around me inside the house.

James can at times be very thoughtless. After I had been to Melbourne at the last gift fair, I flew into Townsville at ten pm. Instead of thinking sensibly and suggesting I stay there overnight, where I could relax and enjoy some girl talk with a friend, he expected me to drive to his parents' home at Charters Towers, arriving there at about midnight. When I suggested staying in Townsville overnight, he sent a text back: *Thought you would so you could avoid us.*

What? My mind boggled as to what that was about.

After twenty years I thought his possessive, selfish insecurities had been extinguished, but no,

I've discovered they still linger. I've always been an independent woman. We had been going out together for about six years when I went overseas. It was no secret that I'd always wanted to travel. The people in my family are mad travellers and the women are all strong-minded.

James's background is very different. His family hasn't travelled much at all, which isn't a bad thing, as not everyone can be so fortunate. But that's no reason for people not to expand their minds in other ways. I received a lot of negative comments from members of his family, such as: 'She can't possibly love him if she's leaving him.'

James's mother still cannot understand why I let James go fishing with his friends, as she and her husband and kids did everything together. It didn't seem to make them any happier, as he and his siblings barely communicate. Also, I can't stand fishing.

William summed it up well when he was about four. We'd gone fishing in a local river for the day and the two oldest ones were fishing with their father. After many hours of waiting and watching, William said, 'Do you know what, Mum? I wish all the fish in the world were dead.'

I just looked at him and smiled. 'Darling, me too.'

It was pure wishful thinking on our part, but at that precise moment we were both totally over this family bonding session. What's the point of trying to enforce a family moment if not all the participants are enjoying it?

Consequently, James goes fishing at least four times a year without us and I'm happy for him to do that. I can't wait for him to get going. I watch him drive out the gate and then life is pretty relaxed for the kids and me. We can have scrambled eggs for tea if we like. I can sit up in bed and read a book as late as I like.

James works very hard in his job and has a lot of day-to-day stress, so it's only fair that he has time away to relax. Fishing is everything to him. He lives and breathes it. He has said that he loves the build-up beforehand, getting everything organised. I feel it's very important for him to enjoy that and to have this time away.

Sadly, I'm not afforded the same courtesy. When I need time out and go away, it's like a mortal sin. I've never been away when he hasn't tried to ruin my moment in some subversive way, either by making a smart-arse comment, or being sulky on the phone. And I can't even let him know that I'm having a nice time away. God forbid I might actually be having fun.

My mother says I married my father in that regard. Dad acted the same way with her whenever she went home to visit her parents. He would be sulky the whole time, and as much as I loved and adored my father, I can see him behaving that way.

So that's how it stands. When I do get to have time to myself, I cherish every moment.

When James spends time with his parents, it's usually just long enough for their thoughts and ideas about our relationship, and our children, to affect him. It takes a good couple of weeks for him to get back into the rhythm of how we manage our affairs, or, I should say in all honesty, how *I* like things done. I can be quite rigid and firm, and I stand my ground in how I like things to run. James's mother has a strong, dominant personality and over the years something has happened with the easy-going me of old. She has taken a step back, and a more controlled, stoic, strong side of me has taken a firm foothold.

When we started a family of our own I didn't really know how I was going to navigate this new adventure, but I did know it was going to be *my* way. So I took, and keep taking, the good things from my childhood and I try to improve on what my parents didn't get quite right. Hopefully it makes for a balanced mix. As there's no handbook on life, or raising children, we just have to try and do our very best and hope it's the right path.

Are you in a relationship with someone who ticks all your boxes? It's highly unlikely if you're a Gemini like me. We have so many facets to our personality that only we can decide what's important to us; what we need to have stability and friendship. It's not often Geminis give way to flights of fancy. I would say it's a very blessed woman indeed who's in a relationship with a man who completes every component of her personality.

Many women would *say* they are happy, but are they? Are they really? I don't think so. Often it's not so much that they are unhappy in their relationships, but they may not be getting the fulfilment they get from their closet and dearest friends. Maybe this is why we women have so many different characters in our lives to complete us. With Geminis, however, I don't think we ever fully cover every layer of our personality.

I can usually pick a character with a Gemini personality in a film. For instance, when I watched *The Duchess*, Jean and I both thought the duchess was a Gemini. I Googled the film and, sure enough, the duchess was a Gemini. We can usually pick them.

When reading *Fifty Shades of Grey*, I kept wondering if the male character was a Gemini and, sure enough, he was. I'm not sure if the author had multi-personality Geminis in mind intentionally when forming the character, or whether it was just a fluke, but she sure wrote the character to suit his star sign.

So we Geminis read and surround ourselves with a multitude of varying personalities to try and fulfil us, but in my friend's mum's opinion, no one ever truly knows a Gemini.

What I've learned about personal space is that every single one of my twenty-five personalities requires time out. Life is not that simple or obliging, however, so I've learned to focus on quality rather than quantity. Even if it's just a few minutes, I grab them and make the most of them.

46

Musings

As I take time to reminisce over my life in my fortieth year, I wonder if all is lost. Is it gone? Will it return? Did I ever have it? Or is it simply a misplaced yearning, waiting for me to rediscover it? I'm talking about passion, lust, and hunger for excitement—and not just sex, but my zest for life.

I love my husband, and I am as in love with him as ever. He is my friend, and when all else fails, that's important. When passion has gone missing, you have your love and friendship to keep you moving forward. It may not be the rollercoaster ride we hear about, read about, or see in the movies, but it's a nice steady Ferris-wheel ride.

I never had that mind-blowing passion in my twenties. I was too guarded. I lacked confidence in myself as a sexual being, and I was four years into our relationship before I could relax enough to have an orgasm. I grew up with my mother preaching to hold onto what I had, and not throw it around or offer it as a smorgasbord to just any man. She always said that men don't appreciate 'easy women', and at the end of the night I should thank them for a lovely night and go home with my virtue and integrity intact.

Well, that was easy, as I've been with the same man since I was seventeen, so while all my friends have had more boyfriends than the digits on their hands and feet combined, I am still on a single digit.

Don't get me wrong. I partied just as hard as everyone else, and drank and danced with the best of them, but when a hot guy was trying to chat me up, I didn't let it go any further than flirting. I couldn't really understand why they were bothering in the first place.

During my twelve months overseas I did not have sex with one single man. It wasn't for the lack of guys trying, and it wasn't that I wasn't tempted. There was just something that always held me back.

Between the years of eighteen and twenty-eight I made the most of the good times. Then the sacrifices of motherhood came easily. It didn't matter to me if there were four years between boozy nights out on the razzle-dazzle.

Then my thirties arrived. By then I was a responsible mother and wife. No longer did I go out dancing or drinking, which was fine, as I firmly believe in completing each phase of life. I'm not constantly looking over my shoulder, wondering what might have been.

Life doesn't seem to change for men, however, and God forbid we should remind them that they're fathers. It can seem to them like we're cutting their throats, which at times would be a godsend.

But now something has happened to me. I've entered the new thirties and it's like something has woken in me. Is it a silent midlife crisis? I don't know. All I do know is that whatever it is has to stay silent and stay deep down. I could never admit that I long for some passion, desire and lust in my life. If I admit that to anyone, they'll start looking at me like I've turned into a crazy woman ready to jump the first guy that comes along.

Maybe that's not a bad idea ... but no, I'm not looking to have an affair, or even a one-night stand. (What are those anyway?) But I finally feel desirable. I feel the confidence that I lacked in my twenties, but if I mention that to my friends—even my closest friends—I can see them thinking that my marriage is in trouble, and that I'm thinking of leaving James to play up.

That couldn't be further from the truth. I just feel perpetually horny. Some passionate being deep inside me longs to be ravished and taken to new heights of pleasure. On the odd occasion I do go out, I finally feel I can hold my own among beautiful, desirable women, not in a slutty way, but in a sensual and spiritual way.

I lay the blame on novels like *Fifty Shades of Grey*. Those books are infectious. I've heard it said about books like this that they've been written so well they've awoken hidden desires in women. In reality, a hot, sexy billionaire is not hanging out on every corner panting to performing all kinds of kinky fuckery with us, but there's nothing wrong with the fantasy.

It's our fantasies that keep us women going as we deal with the ever-revolving reality of daily life. If women were brutally honest, there wouldn't be one alive today who wouldn't admit to a desire for some intensely sexy, passionate man to have their wicked way with them in an elevator, or over a piano. Woo-hoo!

Something has taken possession of me lately and I blame it on the storylines of *Vampire Diaries*, *Game of Thrones* and *Spartacus*. Every movie I watch has a deep love story, where sex and passion are one. Unlike my friends who had watched *Vampire Diaries* before me, it's not the hot sexy character of Damon that turns me on; it's the passionately intense character of Stefan that draws me in.

One of my favourite movies is *A Destiny of her Own*. It's about an Italian courtesan who forged her place in Venice at a time when men were considered to be superior, unless a woman became a courtesan, but not just any old courtesan. The central character had men of all levels of power holding her in high regard, as her mind was just as stimulating as her body.

I am not a feminist as such, but I am not submissive either. My husband has always maintained that women have a goldmine between their legs. I'm aware of this, and I think he's right. When used appropriately, in marriage or in life, our 'goldmine' can mean the difference between happiness and unhappiness, success and failure, and love and hatred.

Another vulgar term I've heard over the years is the 'power of the pussy'. As coarse as that term may be, how many men from all walks of life have ruined their lives by allowing an alluring woman to trap them, like a fly in a Venus flytrap? And if women are honest, how many wives or girlfriends would admit that they use their powerful tool to get what they want? I know I have, many times. Men are such simple creatures. They blind themselves to the manipulation of women using that mine of gold.

I am forty. It doesn't matter how many times I repeat that to myself and call it 'the new thirties', I have to accept that I am forty, and that it's taken this long for my sexuality to emerge. Who knows how long it will last? The important thing is that I have finally bloomed.

Why didn't it happen when I had a hot, size-ten body with pert, size-C breasts, I ask myself, instead of now when I'm size F, and have a mummy-tummy that pushes me up to wearing size-fourteen clothes? I have great legs and my butt is okay, but after having four caesarean births my abdominal muscles are train wrecks.

I'm determined that my body is going to join the ride now that I've bloomed sexually, emotionally and spiritually, however long it takes to knock it into shape. I don't have access to personal trainers or the time to attend a gym, but I can still transform the mummy-tummy with what tools I have available to me at home, using sheer bloody determination.

So what does this mean? I ask myself. Where do I go from here?

And the answer comes back to me: nowhere.

I'll continue harbouring deep-seated burning passions, but nothing will change. I know and accept that this is just a phase in my life. Maybe it's common, and it's just something that happens when women enter the new thirties. I'll continue to mentally lust after and desire fictional characters, if that's what helps me be the best mother and wife I can be. I'm not entirely sure how I succeed on either of those fronts, but I try.

Acknowledgements

Thank you, Rosa, for reading and organising my very first manuscript, as it was a shocker.

I would also like to thank those friends and family who offered unwavering words of encouragement and always believed in me, and this book, especially during those times when I doubted myself.

To my friends and family, thank you for continuing to be a part of my journey. It's been quite a bumpy ride.

I would like to thank my husband for his continual support. Even though he thinks I was mad for writing a book like this, he still says, 'Well done.'

To the power of attraction that eventually showed me the way to the Book Cover Cafe. It was amazing. And I want to thank my editor, with whom I felt an instant connection. She boosted my confidence and ironed out the wrinkles, and her insights were invaluable.

Lastly, I'm grateful for that hopeful feeling inside me that constantly reminds me that everything will work out in the end, even when things look bleak. It tells me: stay positive!

For more info and updates visit:
www.gidgeebaskets.com

www.ingramcontent.com/pod-product-compliance
Lightning Source LLC
Chambersburg PA
CBHW071909290426
44110CB00013B/1341